Harold —   8/2003
Think you'll
enjoy my cousin's
story.

Lou

9=HL

AF339290

Our Blood and His Guts!

(Memoirs of One of General Patton's Combat Soldiers)

Tech. Sgt. Eugene W. Luciano

Library of Congress Catalog Card Number 95-71135

ISBN Number   1-57087-187-6

Production design by Robin Ober

Professional Press
Chapel Hill, NC 27515-4371

Manufactured in the United States of America
96 95 94 93 92   10 9 8 7 6 5 4 3 2 1

To My Wife Mary
Encouragement She Gave
My Parents Antonio & Luisa
Who Were Always There For Their Children
To My Son-In-Law And My Daughter
Richard & Katherine
For Giving Me
My Four Grandchildren

Acknowledgements

I am indebted to the following people:

My deep and sincere thanks to my nephew David Mazzaferro for his expertise, editing and time spent in the writing of these memoirs.

Also to Wayne and Susan Baylis Sposato for their help in setting up pictures and graphics.

Contents

Prologue

This work is not a history or a biography, but recollections and some opinions of my army life during WW II. It is a remembrance of events as accurately as I can remember and what I believe of a civilian soldier along with others serving his country during the 2nd World War by attacking the evil Nazi Empire.

After writing these memoirs about a long time ago, there may be some places and times that may not be perfectly accurate. I tried to recollect as best as I could from memory. When I first entered the army it was to serve and do the time and return home, but everything changed that - the War and Pearl Harbor.

The friends one makes in the army are different than everyday acquaintances. The comraderie of your buddies become part of your life and soon in combat you'll do anything to help, even the sacrifice of ones life as they would do for you. Many gave the supreme sacrifice to save their army buddies.

Many Germans were drafted, as we were, to fight for their own country. One of the first German divisions that we fought was the Elite 17SS Panzergrendiers at Raids in Normandy and also later on at the breakthrough on July 26, 1944.

The defenses of the Atlantic Wall were under Field

Marshal Rundstedt's command and under the direction of General Rommel. They both disagreed on how to setup the defense of their divisions. Rommel wanted them closer to the beach to stop the invasion on the shores, but to do this, they would have to spread out their divisions. The Germans had about 60 divisions in the west. There were only six divisions holding Normandy, four of which were in the coastal area and also protecting the Pas De Calais shore where the Germans expected the main Allied landing.

Field Marshal Rundstedt wanted to keep his divisions in reserve and smash the Allies with strength at the point of invasion. Rundstedt told his chief of staff that the first 24 hours would be decisive for success or failure. When the attack came, much of the German armor was held back believing that this was not the real attack. They believed the attack would be at Pas De Calais.

An Allied ploy was to leak information that General Patton was concentrating his army to attack the Pas De Calais area by displaying much activity in the Dover area and heavy bombing at Pas De Calais. This decision was a major blunder by the German command which allowed the Allies to get a solid beachhead in Normandy. The Germans were holding two key pivotal points, St. Lo and Caen. They both fell after fierce fighting. St. Lo was pounded into rubble and was taken on July 8th and Caen fell on July 10th, 1944.

The hedgerows were an obstacle that the Germans had zeroed in. Movement was difficult until our tanks with steel prongs welded to their frames, cut through the roots, dirt, and branches of the thick bocage.

Operation Cobra started on July 25th with a heavy aerial bombardment and a 1st Army breakthrough from St. Lo. Our 4th Arm'd Division was part of the spearhead and advancing and capturing Coutances, Avranches, and Rennes. The 4th Arm'd was now part of the 3rd Army under Patton, "Old Blood and Guts!" The soldiers heard of his daring and troubles in Africa. They heard of the bloody mess at the Kasserine Pass, the victories and at a hospital the slapping of a battle fatigued soldier when the GI said, "I can't take it anymore!", and also in the invasion of Sicily and Patton's obsession to capture Messina before General Montgomery. We heard of his great beliefs in having fought in most of the great battles in ancient times. This is the man who is now in charge of our destiny and is rumored to have boasted, "I am going to Berlin and kick that Schickel-Gruber right in the ass and kill the bastard!", causing many of us to say, "Sure, Our Blood, His Guts!"

The successful actions by the Breakthrough into the Brittany Peninsula, so upset Hitler, he replaced Rundstedt with General Van Kluge. Hitler ordered Van Kluge to make a counter-attack at Mortain cutting through to Avranches and to the sea, thus cutting off our supply lines. The German attack failed and they were annihilated. The carnage was devastating. For days, the bodies of bloated soldiers, horses, wagons, guns and vehicles, were a horrible sight. Van Kluge did not have enough soldiers and equipment to make that attack as he had to send some of his forces to hold British and Canadian forces coming down from Caen. The slowness of General Mongomery's failure to close the Falaise Gap allowed many German soldiers to escape the trap. General Patton requested to make a right hook with his troops, but was denied because it could have caused a mix-up of armies without a clear dividing line between them. Hitler sacked Van Kluge for the failure of his counter-attack and replaced him with General Walter Mondel. Field Marshal Rundstedt was put back in charge of the Western front.

The 4th Arm'd Division continued their march to the French ports of Vannes, St. Nazaire, and Lorient. This action irked our General Wood with General Patton, saying "We are fighting this war in the wrong direction and we should be attacking towards Paris and eastward."

The 4th Arm'd Division bypassed many strong points, cutting off their supplies and took many prisoners. General Wood wanted to move at a quicker pace than Patton. Much success and credit for the advancement should be given to "Tiger Jack" General Wood.

The 4th Arm'd Division raced eastward taking Orleans, St. Dizier, Sens, Troyes, Commercy, Nancy, Luneville, Arracourt, and right up to the Saar in Alsace Lorraine. We never understood why Patton sacked General Wood, but it was rumored that Patton thought that Wood was tired and needed a rest because of

Wood's request to give his division a respite after 87 days in combat.

My assumption is that Patton wanted all the glory for himself. Generals were always looking for big reports and headlines in newspapers.

The end of the war was in sight until a colossal misjudgment of the Allied High Command sending all supplies to Montgomery's armies for his attack at Arnhem and the Rhine Bridges. This prevented the 3rd and 7th Armies from attempting the crossing the Rhine into Germany and ending the war.

The last major battle at Bastogne beginning on Dec. 16, 1944, was the finish of any hope for the Germans and it marked the victory for the Allies. The war would continue for another six months and many more brave men would die on each side until the end.

About The Author

Eugene W. Luciano, Serial No. 31048909, was born in Torrington, Connecticut on April 20, 1916. He was a Technical Sergeant (Platoon Sgt.) Co. F 51st; Co. "C" & "A"; 10th Armored Infantry Battalion, 4th Armored Division. Drafted July 9, 1941. Discharged October 26, 1945. Served at Camp Devens, Mass., did basic training at Camp Croft, S.C., and was shipped to Pine Camp, N.Y. for armored training on October 25, 1941. His next assignment, maneuvers at Camp Forrest, Tenn. began on October 2, 1942 and he went on to desert maneuvers at Camp Young, Calif. on November 17, 1942. Shipped out June 13, 1943 to serve at Camp Bowie (Brownwood, TX)and Fort Hood (Dallas, TX) and left for the Port of Embarkation on December 20, 1943 at Myles Standish in Massachusetts. He sailed from Boston for overseas duty December 29, 1943 and landed at the Firth of Wales to Devizes, England on January 11, 1944. Was stationed at Chippenham, England, leaving for Utah Beach, France July 9, 1944 and arrived there July 13, 1944.

Awards: 5 Battle Stars ETO; Army Commen-dation Medal; Purple Heart w/Oak Leaf Cluster; Bronze Star; Certificate of Merit; American Campaign; American

Defense; Combat Infantry Badge; Victory Medal; Germany Occupation Medal; and Good Conduct Medal.

Unit Awards: Presidential Citation and Croix De Guerre.

Wounded slightly on patrol at Arracourt, France September, 1944 and at Fenetrange in November, 1944 and returned to duty in a fortnight.

Greatest Achievements: Normandy and Arracourt patrols and outposts; helped to secure the Ducey Dams; led the attack and capture of a German platoon at Luneville; led an attack on St. Genevieve and also the outskirts of Jena, Germany; helped in the reorganization of Co. "A" 10 A.I.B. with Capt. Adrian Tessier after the failed mission of Capt. Baum's raid to rescue Col. John Waters, Gen. Patton's son-in-law; many times a platoon leader due to combat circumstances.

Declined a battlefield commission in December at Alsace-Lorraine and accepted a Merit 30 day furlough stateside.

Education: Graduated Torrington High School, 1934; Newspaper Institute of America for Creative Writing; Trade and Civil Service Correspondence Courses.

Sports and Game Awards: About 1929, Torring-ton YMCA City Checker Tournament Champion, led

Basketball Wonder A.C. to Boy's City Championship; led Basketball Wonder A.C. to Senior City Championship; played with Gleason's and Sacred Heart Champion Ball Clubs; led the City League in Batting Averages.

Founded Luciano's Dry Cleaners in 1947.

Married Mary L. Kostak on February 12, 1949, one daughter Katherine and four grandchildren.

Clubs and Organizations: Past President and Chairman of the Northeast Chapter of the 4th Armored Division Veterans;Life Member of the following organizations, Military Order of the Purple Heart; B.P.O.E. Elks; Northeast Chapter, 4th Armored Division Veterans; 704th Tank Battalion Veterans; Military Museum of Southern New England States, American Legion, Veterans Of Foreign Wars, Concordia Lodge, Sons Of Italy; 3rd and 4th Degrees, Knights of Columbus; Member of Dixie Chapter, New York Chapter, 4th Armored Division; F. O. Eagles, and St. Peters Holy Name Society.

Our Blood and His Guts!

by

Tech. Sgt. Eugene W. Luciano

Edited

by

David J. Mazzaferro, Sr.

1st Edition: May, 1995

Chapter I

Remembrances

From the town of Chippenham to the loading of half-tracks and tanks full with equipment and supplies to the port of embarkation at the Port of Southampton where LST's and LCI's were waiting to be loaded. Although the loading would be delayed for a time until the beachhead could be enlarged in Normandy – we were tented for a few days before boarding ship.

In those few days – canisters of poisonous gases could be seen stockpiled for any eventuality that couldn't be avoided due to the enemy, to be used at a moment's notice.

Many were the days before these preparations that maneuvers were held to hone the fighting skills of the men.

Many were the times the outfit would be on patrol to protect the southern shores of English coastline – Plymouth, Torquay, Southampton, so the Navy could go about their business of preparing for the invasion which was called "Overlord".

There was no time to be scared – it was an adventure to make history and the so-called "Peace in our time for all time".

Many times squadrons of bombers could be seen in formation ready to attack the fortress of Europe in the dusk of night.

During these times – soldiers were restricted to the Quonset huts and the compound so no information or any slip could provide any clue to unfriendly eyes about our activities.

At this time we were given orders to sew into our combat jackets, a silk map of Europe and a small compass between the lining and the outer shell of the jacket. This was in any event that arose from any eventuality as a prisoner of war or getting lost or separated from the unit so to return to our friendly lines.

Passwords were issued and changed every day to be used when challenged by sentries or by anyone entering friendly lines. We also were issued cricket clickers to be used for movements and unknown noises to identify and contact our friendly forces, especially at night. One click had to be answered by two sharp clicks for identification and contact. One night, outside of Luneville on high ground below the crest of the hill, I heard some noises above us and I made a clicking noise. I heard no answer except for muffled sounds that sounded foreign. I quickly pulled a pin out of a grenade and threw it at the sound, hollering, "Grenade!" to alert my squad to take cover. The rest of the night became quiet.

It was very frustrating, especially when appointments and dates were made that could not be kept.

The storming of the French beaches was

imminent and the beginning of the end was at hand.

After a few days, the division was set on its way to its destiny. D-Day was history and the beachhead was secured.

Sailing in the channel was exciting. Planes were overhead with an occasional dogfight, there were sights of a parachute in the sky and a tail of smoke from a falling plane.

V-bombs were falling haphazardly in English cities and they could be seen in their flight.

In the waters offshore of the French coast, there were boats to be unloaded and men waiting for the tide to go out so they could disembark.

The vehicles at low tide, with all parts of the engine impregnated (waterproofed), hit the water onto the French shores of Normandy.

Bodies of men in the water from earlier engagements and cans and equipment could be seen floating in the water. Also launches were bringing supplies from supply ships to the shore.

Once the outfit was ashore and in column with half-tracks, tanks, and supply trucks, this marked the beginning of the end of the German conquest of the world .

On the march to the bivouac area near La Margerie and Raids (or Perriers) beyond St. Mere Eglise, France into a field in which the vehicles circled the field – the men dismounted and rested a short time – and then the rains soaked everything.

The Allied beaches and occupation territory were

very crowded with troops, vehicles and supplies. A larger movement to capture more area to land and to store more supplies was needed. There were 2 1/2 million men and 1/2 million vehicles of all kinds already landed and waiting for an opportunity to break out of the lodgement area.

Our air power was mainly responsible for keeping the enemy from building up their forces to attack our positions. We were in a defensive position and the land of farm's hedgerows caused many problems restricting the use of our armor. Many of the armored soldiers were used in defense resulting in casualties of the armored force's highly trained men which we could not afford to lose.

The enemy had all the hedgerows zeroed in for any movement and their fire was very accurate.

General Montgomery was in charge of all ground forces and the plans on the battlefield and it was his tendency to be overly cautious that was delaying the breakout of our lodgement area. His failure to take the objective, the city of Caen, caused much alarm at Supreme Headquarters. Later, when the city was taken, a plan was to carpet-bomb with a massive attack to the Caen front for a breakout. General Montgomery's many delays in attacking were a disappointment to the Allied Command. His idle boast that the events of the war were going according to plan, irked the general staff and Winston Churchill.

When General Bradley devised his "Cobra" operation for a breakout of our lodgement area, it became a success. General Montgomery claimed the attack on his front caused the German's General Model to send most of the enemy troops to his (Montgomery's) immediate front. This action he claimed, caused the weakening of the German lines at Bradley's front creating an opportunity for a successful breakout. Montgomery implied that he deserved credit for his action.

Most of the future manpower and supplies were from the United States as Great Britain was hard-pressed to provide them because of its many years of carrying the war alone.

General Montgomery's overall strategy was to make a large scale attack in the North and take the port of Antwerp and drive into the Ruhr to the Rhine River and into the heart of Germany, thus causing the downfall of the Nazi Empire and the end of the war. This plan was denied by Eisenhower because of the difficulty of protecting the flanks of the operation

Many supplies, vehicles, and manpower would have to be sacrificed from the Third and Seventh Army Campaigns causing these armies problems to defend and move against the enemy in the South. General Eisenhower decided to attack on a solid broad front with air cover and no flanks exposed.

Patton's armies disregarded the flanks and with air cover, moved so swiftly, we were 150 miles beyond the Seine River line by September 1st. The plan had been only to reach the Seine River by that date. This caused logistics problems and we also had to fight off many counterattacks in the Alsace-Lorraine Campaigns as our flanks became exposed. However, our mobility and air cover beat back the counter-attacks.

This is how I remembered it:

Some lieutenant ordered us in a skirmish line (same as policing the area in an encampment) with drawn bayonets to poke into the ground for mines as we moved forward from one end of the field to the other. Poking the bayonet into the ground a few inches forward each time – he had us so close together that if a mistake was made, many injuries and deaths would have occurred. If we saw cows grazing in the fields, it suggested that the area was clear of mines, also to be on alert if the cows were staring and still, looking in one direction, warning us of any unknown activity.

When the rains came – many of the men congregated under the trees.

This was when most of the men discarded equipment – such as impregnated clothes (used in case of gases) and buried it in the ground.

The field kitchen truck served us a meal in the field, the last that I could remember until September – 87 days in the line continuously – a long time on C rations. C rations were easy to carry, the box was 2 by 6 inches long. Ten and ones (rations) were in the half-track. The front line troops subsisted on these rations, but rear echelon had hot food as a kitchen was always with the top brass. I can remember only one hot meal in the field during a lull in the action. Our job was to advance and attack, take the objective, then take the high ground while the brass and service people billeted in town with hot meals.

With a little bit of sarcasm, if you remember when the massacre of our troops at the Battle of Ardennes (Battle of the Bulge), the top brass were back at headquarters, well dressed, with white tablecloths, orderlies at their beck and call, the best of food, while the boys were dying on the front. Not many of the top brass, received injuries in the rear echelons except, if they cut themselves while cutting-up their meals and with their medals hanging down their front for deeds that the men accomplished and some died for.

I can't say enough for the junior officers in the front lines. They paid their dues. Many died bravely carrying out their assignments. I admired and respected all my junior officers who led their men along with their non-commissioned officers. Another group of men that deserve praise and glory, were those of the Red Ball Express bringing up supplies to the front lines. There were many obstacles in carrying out their duties such as strafing by the Luftwaffe, mined roads or by German spies and sympathizers. Then, there are the pilots who gave ground support, dropped supplies through ack-ack and ground fire. We owe a debt of gratitude for these acts of bravery and courage. How about the Chaplains who gave hope and sacrifice of their lives to spare others? These dedicated men should never be forgotten. To those who profited and operated in "black markets", prospering and living in opulence, deserve no gratitude nor respect.

On the battlefield, I saw brave men dying! I saw them crying! I saw mangled bodies! I saw the hungry children! I saw abused people and battle fatigued soldiers! I saw the misery in concentration camps! I saw happy faces of a well accomplished mission! I saw boys become men!

War is hell for what it does to life and property. We have free will to do good. Let's use it and live with each other, and settle our disputes peacefully. "C'est la vie!"

The men were grumbling to get moving and soon they got their wish.

The training was so extensive and complete with all possible conditions that could occur in combat.

On September 1, 1939 little did I know that from this day forward, the lives of all the world's people would change.

Germany attacked Poland; England and France declared war on Nazi Germany. All previous attempts to appease Hitler were fruitless. Even allowing the march into the Ruhr, the annexation of Sudetenland, the fall of Austria, and the taking of Czechoslovakia failed to stop the German blitzkrieg.

The treaty between England, France and Poland had to be honored. An attack on any one of them would be an act of war.

The fall of Poland was quick and decisive. The German army turned to the west into their Seigfried Line facing the French in the Maignot Line. It was a time of waiting through the winter, for fighting was at a standstill and later it was dubbed a "Phony War". A year or so later the "Fall of France" and the evacuation of the British troops from the beaches at Dunkirk occurred.

In the United States, the military drafting of young men was into law in 1940 and the first draft number was #158. My number was drawn in February, 1941 and I was to be called up on a later day. I received my orders with a letter stating, "Greetings!" and it said I would be inducted into the Army on July 9. 1941.

I was employed as a tool maker in The Hendey Machine Lathe Company. The company would have given me a deferment, but I thought I would have to enlist later so I decided to put in my year of military service and then get on with my life. I was about 25 years of age. My parents gave me some parties and gatherings with friends and relatives. The Hendey Machine Co. gave me a carton of cigarettes and $50 dollars. My parties brought in another $50 dollars.

My cousin Arthur Compito, who was living with us, decided to go in with me. Although he had a later induction date, he was accepted into the Army at this time. After all the medical tests were passed by Dr. Pratt, I was fit to be entered in the army. Can you believe I passed the tests so conveniently, but when I was working, my Dr. Weed kept me coming back to him every month for examinations. Now all of a sudden, I'm in A-1 condition.

I was born April 20, 1916 in Torrington, Connecticut of Italian parentage. In my early years, I always strived to be the best I could be in whatever I was doing. If I could not reach that goal, I would move on to something else. I had the wanderlust!

My father came from a small town called Curti in the hills above Salerno, Italy. His father was a land baron who was in business making and selling charcoal. He loved his son, but was very strict, so his grandmother took him in and raised him. as his mother died during childbirth. In his school years, my father would explain to us children, the harshness and punishment of the teachers when some pupils did not understand or pay attention.

At the age of fourteen, hearing of America, the land of opportunity, with the remarks that, "The streets are paved in gold", he desperately wanted to go. Earning a little money and with the help of his grandmother, he saved enough money to sail to America at the age of seventeen. He booked passage in the ship's steerage, leaving behind his loved ones and a girl named Louise. Passing through Ellis Island in 1903, a relative brought him to the Scranton and Wilkes-barre area to work in the coal mines. After 3 years, in 1906, getting lonely, he returned to Italy and married his sweetheart Louise, my mother. The best thing my father did besides rearing me up was coming to America, which made me an American.

Italians are very warm and loving people, but when they are downtrodden by individuals, their love turns to hate. This is why many underworld societies such as the Mafia got started.

In America, quotas favored the Irish, English, German and Scandinavians. Because of discrimination, there were smaller quotas for the romantics, the blacks, the Jews and orientals, unless they were artisans or intellectuals.

Growing up Italian, I always tried to excel in many activities. When I could not reach perfection, I would try to do other things that interested me. I would say, "Jack-of-all-trades, but master-of-none."

In my early years, I served as an altar boy in church and I was being asked to prepare for the priesthood. Some young men did accept the offer of the church and attend colleges such as Fordham for a free education, but couldn't take that vocation and instead became professionals and businessmen. I couldn't be so deceitful.

When I graduated from Torrington High School in 1934, the country was in a deep depression with many people jobless and on welfare. The future of graduates was very bleak. Having taken college courses in school, I decided to further my education by applying into West Point through my father's friend who was friendly with a Senator. The information came back that I was too short at 5ft 6" and had to be 5ft 7" tall. I couldn't believe it. Was it because I was Italian? How many Italians ever came out of West Point? After working as a dry cleaner and as a machinist, now I understood why I didn't take the deferment that the factory would have given me.

Chapter II

Goodbye Torrington

"**G**REETINGS!" On Wednesday morning July 9, 1941 at 9:00 o'clock, I answered my induction call to Torrington City Hall. A large group met in the courtroom and Mayor Patten gave us a welcoming speech. There were at least 30 of us and I knew many of the young men. We were all excited and during the first few nights when the bugler played and the lights were to be extinguished, we all thought we had to be bedded by 9:00 o'clock. As time went on, we learned we could be anyplace on the post.

The supply sergeant handed out our fatigues and other supplies.

The medical officer gave us shots and a "peter inspection". At this inspection, all of us would form a single line dressed only in a raincoat and shoes. A medical officer would sit on a stool and examine each of us, front and back, a very embarrassing situation.

Only at Fort Devens did I ever do K.P. during my 4 1/2 years in the army. The first weekend I was in the army, my parents and my brother John and his wife Lucy, came to the fort to see me. Boy! Looking back, we must have looked like raw recruits, but I could see that Pop and Mom were proud to have a son serve in the army and that was an honor for my family. In the two weeks at Fort Devens, the time was spent in classes of army procedures, marching, calisthenics and close order drills. Recruits learned very quickly to follow orders, even though sometimes they didn't make sense. This was the army life – do as you're ordered.

Moving on to Spartanburg, Camp Croft, South Carolina by troop train was very exciting. At the Spartanburg railroad station, army trucks were waiting and transported us into a new camp built for the training of citizen soldiers. We were assigned to barracks hap-hazardly. The officers counted out names of the recruits assigned to each barracks. Once we were assigned to a barracks, the rush was hectic for bunks to be close to our new found friends. This was the 33rd Training Battalion.

We were assigned a hardened sergeant from Alabama. With a heavy Southern drawl, he shouted very strict and demanding orders. My thoughts on army life were changing. It seemed that our souls weren't our own because we were always being harassed and bossed. As time went on, we realized that this created a better, disciplined soldier and developed a well trained army.

Inspections of barracks, latrines, bunks, weapons, footlockers, clothing and personal appearance were constant. These were practically impossible to pass without being "gigged". There were many full barrack inspections. All lockers had to be opened and everything in neat array. The bed with the O.D. blanket had to be taught and springy. A speck of dirt or a coin that didn't bounce off the bed's blanket when it was dropped on it or having an untidy bunk area, you went on latrine and garbage details and were restricted to quarters. In the field, there were inspections that the soldiers had to line up outside their tents displaying all of their equipment and standing at attention. There were inspections while we were in platoon formation, for neatness of dress, shoes shined, clean shaven and spotless guns. In the inspection of guns, the officer, wearing white gloves, would inspect each and every gun as each soldier was in the position of "port arms". He would snap the rifle from the soldier as the soldier would let go, turn the rifle, look down the barrel and hand the rifle back to the soldier. A lieutenant, inspecting the platoon, faced me while I was at port arms. Seeing the small movement of his eyes, before he made a grab for my rifle, I let go. The rifle fell to the ground as he made a grab for the inspection. I did not flinch nor move and stayed at attention. After an awkward moment, he stooped and picked up my rifle and handed it back to me with a smirk on his face and continued his inspection. Soldiers were to let go of their rifle as soon as the officer motioned to inspect it. This day, he was a fraction too slow. This was in basic training.

The training was so strenuous that some who could not take the stress, took their own lives. They were making us hardened soldiers.

We had map and compass reading, lectures, nomenclatures and taking apart and assembling all types of weapons and can you believe listening to the "Articles of War" again? We had machine gun training and pistol firing. The non-coms taught us how to hold, aim and squeeze the trigger. "Squeeze it like a lemon," they would shout. At first, we were jerking and pulling on the trigger causing us to miss the targets. We were also taught how to lay a mine field with the idea that at some future time, the mine field would have to be cleared. We would use compasses to get coordinates and make a grid plot-plan and set the mines in a pattern so that they could be located.

I made many friends, visited many places of interest with my closest buddies, Rudolf Hirchak, Arthur Compito, and Sammy Sica. We would go into Spartanburg on weekends, walking the streets, singing and marching now and then to the sound of "ONE, TWO, THREE, FOUR, WHAT ARE WE HERE FOR? HOORAY! HOORAY!" Soldiers fighting in town over female companionship were endless and many soldiers went back to camp with bumps and bruises. The BlueBird Restaurant was our hangout. The three of us, Art, Rudy and I would hitchhike to many places in South Carolina. We would go into Greenville, Union, Gaffney, and the Civil War battlefields at Cowpens. Rudy and I on a weekend at a Greenville hotel met a very interesting young lady who was willing to make our life interesting. Since we had a room at the hotel, we took up her offerings. Rudy did alright, but for some reason she and I called it off. I wasn't firing. She made a few bucks. Later on we saw her on the street with her boyfriend. What a way to make a living.

Wherever there are soldiers, the prostitutes or hookers followed. The word "hookers" came during the Civil War, when General Joseph Hooker brought in prostitutes for his troops. The soldiers called them Hooker's girls and that is where the name is derived from. The same thing applies to sideburns, which originated from soldiers of Rhode Island's General Ambrose Burnside's facial whiskers. In South Carolina at the Greyhound Bus Station, hookers were plying their trade. An occasional taxi driver, acting as a pimp, got tricks for hookers (and sometimes for his girlfriend) to perform the act right in the cab. In California, the prostitutes lingered around nightclubs, bars and U.S.O. Clubs. In England, many hookers propositioned the soldiers on the streets. When one approached and said she had a proposition for me, I did not know what she had in mind. I learned fast! The World War I song, "How can you keep them down on the farm when they've seen Paree" came into my mind and I understood. In France, brothels were legal. Some fancy brothels with all the trappings; music, bar and women in slinky gowns, entertained the soldiers. The lines of soldiers stretched out with intermingling with officers and enlisted men. There was no rank protocol and no bucking the line as was the case in camp in chow lines. In Germany, after the war was won, the females were all easy marks. They were looking for favors such as stockings, chocolates, food and drinks. Many soldiers came down with diseases and went to the infirmary because they failed to use the prophylactics issued by the army. Some who were infected, were caught at "peter" inspection. There was a saying when leaving camp on pass or leave that went, "I am going into town, TO GET STEWED! SCREWED! AND TATTOOED!" How true!

I got a surprise letter from home that my family was coming down to see me and that I was to find accommodations for them in Spartanburg. I located a beautiful home in town for them. They stayed there only one night as the lady said she needed the rooms for others she previously had booked. I later learned, my mother wore her religion on her right arm and being Catholic in a K.K.K. home was the reason for the departure. They located a motel run by friendly people who were very hospitable.

The time came for my family to leave. Parting is always difficult.

Coming back to camp from town on a bus one night, some soldiers were cutting up and I tried to quiet them down and before I could do anything, one drunken soldier slashed my clothes with a knife. Luckily, I jumped back and only received a scratch. Other soldiers separated him from the knife and the event was forgotten.

Chapter III

Pine Camp

After 13 weeks of basic training, we were ordered to go to our new destinations which was Pine Camp in New York State, north of Watertown. They included my friends, Arthur Compito, Armand Pollutro, Patrick Quinn, Paul Persechino, Arthur Pergola and Phillip Cianciola from Torrington . They were placed in different companies. I left Rudy Hirchak, Sam Sica, George Kozlak and Andrew Fusco at Camp Croft.

I was placed in "F" Co, 51st Arm'd Infantry, 4th Arm'd Division. This was a new division activated April 15, 1941. Armored divisions were formed after seeing the lightening thrust of German armored attacks with tanks and armored infantry quickly routing the Allies. The 4th Arm'd Division was formed by cadres from the 1st and 2nd Arm'd Divisions which were activated July 15, 1940. The 1st Arm'd Division Cadre came from Fort Knox, Kentucky. The 2nd Arm'd Division Cadre came from Fort Benning, Ga. The 4th Arm'd Division Cadre formed the 5th Arm'd Division Cadre October 1, 1941. The 4th Arm'd Division and the 5th Arm'd Division Cadres formed the 8th Arm'd Division April 1, 1942. In the early days at Pine Camp we trained without weapons using trucks for tanks and brooms for guns.

Dress parades and passing in review always sent shivers up and down my spine, a patriotic feeling. As the division, carrying the colors and standards in front of the V.I.P. and top brass, the leader of each battalion would salute and command "Eyes Right"! All soldiers except the ones on the extreme right to keep the marchers going straight, would turn their head and eyes to the right as the colors and the battle standards were lowered in a salute. On one fall day, parts of the division also marched in a parade in London, Ontario.

The close order drills were orders such as columns right or left, to the rear march, oblique right or left, forward march, first squad to the right, left or rear march, etc. and about face, right or left face. In my early days this was no problem as I was always in the middle of the platoon marching and trying to stay in step. Later on, because of my size, I was put on the right front (lead). Then it was very funny. I was balled out by the Sgt. as he barked, "Column right." I didn't know how to turn or move and stumbled and screwed up the whole platoon. No one ever showed me or taught me how. I learned quickly to pivot after that incident. In time I considered myself a very good drill Sgt. in Manual of Arms, drills and posting of guards and becoming a first class soldier.

The organization of the 4th Arm'd Division and its attachments consisted of:

10th Armored Infantry Battalion
51st Armored Infantry Battalion
53rd Armored Infantry Battalion
8th Tank Battalion
35th Tank Battalion
37th Tank Battalion
22nd Armored Field Battalion
66th Armored Field Battalion
94th Armored Field Battalion
24th Armored Engineer Battalion
46th Armored Medical Battalion
126th Armored Ordinance Maintenance Battalion
25th Mechanized Cavalry Reconnaissance Squadron
Headquarters and Headquarters Battery
Division Artillery
CCA Headquarters and Headquarters Company
Reserve Command
Division Headquarters Company
144th Armored Signal Company
Trains Headquarters
Headquarters Company
Forward Echelon 4th Armored Division Headquarters
Rear Echelon 4th Armored Division Headquarters
4th Armored Division MP Platoon
4th Armored Division Band
Attached Tank Destroyer Battalions (704th and 811th)
489th Automatic Weapons Battalion

An armored infantry battalion consists of four platoons of rifle, machine gun and mortar squads. Also, there are service and headquarters companies for a total of 1100 enlisted men and about 40 officers. The officers for each battalion are the commanding officer, executive officer, company commanders, and company officers (platoon lieutenants). The non-commissioned officers are Master Sergeant, 1st Sergeant, Technical Sergeant, S/Sgt., Sgt., and Corporals and Private First Class. The three infantry battalions, the 10th, 51st, and 53rd, plus service and headquarters companies totalled approximately 3500 officers and enlisted men. An armored division has about 14,000 men. I was a platoon sergeant (Technical Sgt.) armed with a 30 cal., 16 shot carbine in charge of 55 men and 5 half-tracks. The men were armed with M-1 Garand rifles. Most officers not armed with carbines, usually carried sidearms (Colt 45's). In my early training, I carried a Springfield '03 bolt-action rifle (held 5 rounds). Being left handed, I had to learn to shoot right handed because of the Springfield's bolt action. Later on, I was issued an M-1 Garand semi-automatic rifle (weighed about 9 lbs. and held an 8 round clip). The Thompson sub-machine gun (grease guns) were issued to half-track and tank drivers. They were fired in small bursts, had a short range and were inaccurate. The carbine and the Garand were very accurate at longer ranges. I could fire each rifle either way if I so desired.

Other weapons were the 30 cal. air-cooled and water-cooled machine guns, 50 cal. air-cooled machine guns, 30 cal. Browning Automatic Rifle (BAR), Bangalore torpedoes, grenade launchers and light and heavy mortars which were very effective at targets in defilade positions.

Many officers used Jeeps (Willys) leading convoys, carrying supplies, and when necessary, evacuating a wounded soldier or transporting a prisoner back to the command post for interrogation. Our half-tracks had 2 front wheels and 2 treaded rear "tank' tracks. They were armed with a 50 cal. gun behind the driver and the half-track commander. The half-track carried a squad of 12 men, driver, commander, and 10 armed infantry soldiers. The half-track weighed approximately 10 tons of heavy tank-like steel. They carried water and gas in G.I. cans. There were rails on the outside of the vehicle holding unfused mines. Some half-tracks would tow a 37mm or 57mm canon. The 37mm gun was useless and the 57mm was not much better. A half-track's speed could accelerate up to approximately 45 mph with a range of 100 miles. With their speed the half-tracks could quickly move troops to help clear obstacles for our tanks. When going on an attack and dismounting from the half-track, we would take only what we needed for combat to our objective. All other equipment was left behind in the half-track.

A combat soldier had bandoliers of 30 cal. ammunition, a rifle belt with cartridges, 2 grenades hanging on his belt, a canteen and his weapon and bayonet. If he had to be away from the half-track for any length of time, then he would take his full field equipment of clothing, mess kit with fork, knife and spoon, small shovel and pick for digging foxholes, some "C" rations and toiletries. It was no fun, but the job had to be done.

The foxholes were slit trenches dug by the soldiers to protect themselves from enemy fire and strafing planes. No matter whether water from the rains half filled them, we still jumped into them for protection from the enemy and the Luftwaffe. The Luftwaffe was practically destroyed near the end of the war. Many were shot down in dog-fights and hangars at airfields and planes on the ground were bombed and strafed. These planes were not airborne because of the lack of fuel. What a beautiful sight to see a dogfight and an enemy plane crashing to the ground. Just one less plane to strafe our troops!

The well equipped soldier would go into combat dressed in olive drab (O.D.) clothes, combat suit, combat boots, fatigues and rain gear. A blouse which was an olive drab colored jacket, was worn on dress occasions which was later replaced by a real snazzy Eisenhower jacket. In summertime we dressed in suntans.

Our tanks were light, medium and heavy, manned by a crew of five. The M-3 light tank (Lee & Stuart) had two inch armor plate, with speed, maneuverability, a six man crew, with fire power (75mm gun, 37mm turret gun and three 30 cal. machine guns). They were effective in giving support to ground troops against enemy infantry, but were like tin cans and no match for the Tiger and Panther tanks (manned by a crew of six). The difference between a tanker and an infantry soldier was the tanker had 3 inches of steel protecting him, while an infantry soldier had only his shirt to stop a bullet. The mediums were better, had a greater range, and were mobile. Our best model, the Sherman held their own in close proximity to enemy tanks and were more of a match for the Germans because of their ability to out-maneuver and aim their guns at targets. Their guns were a 30 cal. and 50 cal. machine guns, a bow gun (which could shoot at a 45 degree angle), and a 75mm cannon which was later replaced by a 76mm cannon. they had 3 inch thick armor and had a top speed of 25 mph with a crew of 5 men (driver, bow gunner, gunner, loader, and commander). The cannons fired armor piercing and exploding incendiary shells. The German tanks had heavier gauge steel armor, whereas our tanks had to be closer to inflict damage to their tanks because many shells from a distance would bounce off their thick armor.

Tank destroyers were highly effective with great speed and gave a good account of their actions. They had light armor to protect from machine gun, fragmentations and rifle fire. They should have been used sparingly, but when needed, they were used against tanks. They were like a cat going after a dog.

At camp, our billets were barracks and Nissen Huts (Quonset Huts), but in the field we had pyramid and pup tents. The shelter half of the tent sometimes was used at night time by soldiers as a cover (to mask the light) at the front to check a map by flashlight for the next day's objective. In camp the barracks had two wide-open floors and many windows. At the end of each floor there was a room that was occupied by the platoon Sgt. on the 1st floor and on the 2nd floor, by the mess Sgt. and his aide. The latrine with many toilets, urinals and wash stands in perfect alignment was located at the other end of the barracks. There were two doors on each floor with fire escapes from the 2nd floor. There was also an inside stairway. There was a boilerroom to make hot water and potbelly stoves to heat the barracks. When we left Pine Camp we were ordered to send all of our civilian clothes home. Mickey Dwyer and I had the bright idea to hide our clothes in the ceiling rafters and retrieve them at some other time. Fifty (50) years later, returning to the camp for a get-together with Mathew Grbovac, for curiosity sake I checked the barracks, but the clothes were gone! In England, the billets were Nissen Huts, all on one floor with double decker beds. These huts were long rounded buildings, housing a platoon.

The patch of the 4th Arm'd Division is triangular with three colors. The blue segment signifies the Arm'd Infantry, the yellow the Cavalry, the red the Artillery, and the cannon and the tank track signifies artillery, tanks and the general's command. The red bolt, a lightening strike, represented shock action by our troops. The Companies practiced exercises throwing ropes across rivers to move men and equipment. One of these was the Black River. The basic tactics of an armored division consist of three combat commands, CCA, CCB, and CCR. Usually, CCA and CCB attacks on each side of enemy flanks and pierces the enemy lines and drive inward and meet and encircles the area penetrated. CCR would rush into where it is needed most to complete the mission. This encirclement has a demoralizing effect on the enemy. The area is then mopped up by the infantry division (foot soldiers). The armored infantry is used mainly to protect the heavy equipment and tanks. If the situation calls for cleaning out nests of anti-tank guns, obstacles for tanks or dangerous river crossings, the armored infantry leads. The tanks should protect the infantry and lead when small enemy infantry units, artillery or mine fields lay ahead.

We had field maneuvers into the towns of Black River, Antwerp, Great Bend, Philadelphia, Carthage and the expansive fields of the camp. We would be out all day. The kitchen truck would serve hot meals. If the weather changed, we would return to our barracks. This was the easiest time of my army life. The winter possibilities of warfare took place in Pine Camp in northern New York state through Plattsburg from our home base located north of Watertown. The long convoy march up through the Adirondacks during the winter of 1941 was to see how an armored division could face the elements of the cold and snow in a combat situation. The 4th Arm'd Division was the first to train in winter conditions. The weather was extremely cold as we traveled in convoy. The convoy would halt many times, in simulated combat exercises and also for a 10 minute break to allow the soldiers to stretch and relieve themselves. At Tupper Lake in the mountains, we crawled into our bedrolls for a night's rest with guards posted around the bivouac area. The temperature was in the teens, but we survived and learned. Continuing along the Hudson River into Plattsburg, we enjoyed a few days in brick buildings which were once the headquarters of the Revolutionary War Army. Moving on through the mountains in convoy in war-like conditions, we crossed many miles across New York State to reach the waters of the St. Lawrence River passing through Massena and down to the Thousand Islands. The scenery, with many small islands was majestic at Alexandria and Clayton, New York. It was a sight to behold! I bought many souvenirs and sent them home. I was enthralled with the beauty of the landscape. On some free time, the boat ride between the islands and visiting Boldt Castle was thrilling. It was a castle that was never finished as construction was halted because of the death of the man's wife and sweetheart. We maneuvered across a small bridge on a small island between Canada and the United States. We bivouacked on the island for a day and then headed back to Watertown and Pine Camp.

The winter – at times – would dip many degrees below zero. The men slept on these maneuvers in bedrolls on the frozen ground -a far cry from the red soil of Camp Croft, South Carolina at Spartanburg during the 13 weeks of boot training.

The ease of getting furloughs and passes (before the hostilities) ended when the war began for America with the attack on Pearl Harbor. When my brother

Ray's upcoming marriage to Loretta in April 18, Art Compito and I asked for and received special permission for leave as we were both to be participants in the wedding. It was a great wedding and for our being in uniform, it felt terrific. We had a great time.

The men who were billeted in barracks now were ordered into the fields in tents – rain or shine. When the exercises – before the breakout of war – were held and it had rained or snowed or any inclement weather, orders were to return to the barracks. The men would never be in barracks again until they arrived in Texas and England and be housed in Nissen Huts. The tents were what we called Pup tents. Each soldier would carry one shelter half and would double with another to put up a pup tent.

The pyramid tents were six to eight cots and they were comfortable. These were in Camp Young, Camp Ibis, California but all this was much later.

There was much free time at Pine Camp from our very easy training before the war. Cards, dice and all kinds of games were played. The Post Exchanges (PX) had great bargains. On weekends, if there was no duty to perform, we could leave the camp. I never shirked guard duty, but Kitchen Police (KP) I avoided. If my name was on the bulletin board for (KP) duty, I would pay a stand-in a fee to take my place for the weekend. Bed checks were very few and far between. On weekends my bunk was always made up. At the camp. I would get my clothes pressed by Mickey Dwyer and haircuts by Montell. They both charged 15 cents.

When I didn't have a pass to leave the post, I would sneak out with Clifford Rowe. We were well acquainted with two sales girls from the (PX) who had a car. I would get into the trunk of the car and we would get past the guard post and go to Lowville to a roadhouse, have dinner, listen to music and return to camp. The sales girls were much older than Cliff and me. His date was on the heavy side and mine was homely, but why complain, it was fun and relaxation. Later on I talked them into a ride to Connecticut and drop me off in my hometown.

Mel Mills had a car at Pine Camp and on weekends we would go home. He lived in the Worcester area. Adrian Tessier, who lived in Providence, also was with us. We pooled our gas rations and I paid a small fee. Speeding home from camp sometimes, we were chased by police, but Tessier always lost them with his reckless driving. They would leave me in Pittsfield and I would hitchhike home and on returning my brother Mario would take me back to Pittsfield. I would hitchhike to Albany and catch a cab to Utica and from there, another cab or bus to camp. At many other times, Pvt. Maas from Maine had a car and we would go into Cornwall, Canada. I was there on Dec. 7, 1941 when the Japanese attacked Pearl Harbor and we were ordered to return immediately to our outfit. All our training at Pine Camp completed – it was time to move on.

Chapter IV

Tennessee, Desert, and Texas Maneuvers

In late September, the soldiers, with a duffel bag over their shoulders, with full equipment were marched to the train station and boarded the trains. The vehicles and heavy equipment were anchored on flat cars. We were on our way for the Tennessee maneuvers starting in early October. Arriving at our destination at Tulahoma, Tenn., we were loaded onto 2 1/2 ton trucks to be transported to Shelbyville where we bivouacked for a few days. All I can remember is mud, mud, mud! While in this area, I was appalled at the treatment of Negroes. Restrooms were separated and also the blacks were to step out of the way of any approaching white person. At that time, no one cared about this injustice. Some of the best soldiers and aides came from these blacks. We left this area for Camp Forrest, mounted on our half-tracks and tanks. The camp was named in honor of Nathan Bedford Forrest, a Confederate general from Tennessee. The rains turned the red clay into gooey mud that created a mess on all our equipment. There was no way anyone could pass an inspection, spot clean. The maneuvers were through the towns, east of Nashville. Crossing the Cumberland river, pontoon bridges were built by the engineers and soldiers attacking through fields of field corn would cross the river on rubber rafts that were transported to the river banks. This was the simulated Red Army against the Blue. Many were the times at night when the troops were lost and had to await for the sunrise to reorganize. This training helped immensely in warfare as we learned more map and compass reading. And so it was. This was September of 1942 and we belonged to the Second Army commanded by Lieutenant General Benjamin Lear. There was no love between the Generals Lear and Wood. In these maneuvers, Gen. Wood believed that an armored division should breech an enemy line and spread out, whereas Gen. Lear thought the maneuvers should go at a slower pace. Speaking in front of the troops, he complained that the tactics were all wrong and that the non commissioned officers were stupid. This infuriated Gen. Wood and he asked to speak in front of his officers and explained that General Lear did not know what he was talking about. Gen. Lear told him to get off the floor and from this heated exchange, other officers defused the situation. This action by Gen. Wood endeared him to his troops for standing up for them. Gen. Wood never took a back seat to anyone, not even General Patton. If Gen. Patton roared, Gen. Wood would roar right back. I believe this boldness on Gen. Wood's part was the cause of his dismissal in December, 1944 by Gen. Patton and sent back to the United States for the command at Ft. Knox Kentucky, training soldiers. Gen. Patton claimed that Gen. Wood needed a rest.

The people of Tennessee were very friendly and would take us into their homes. One night my squad lost our direction and waited until early morning outside a small store. When the owner of the store saw a bedraggled group, he took us to his home for a real southern breakfast of ham, grits and cornbread. I believe this was Gallatin, the home of Sgt. York of WW I fame.

When maneuvers were to travel open roads, we saw many historic sites such as the Hermitage – Jackson's home near Gallatin, Tennessee; the Grand Ole Opry at Nashville, the colleges – Vanderbilt and the University of Tennessee.

When we first arrived in September by troop train, we transferred to half-tracks and tanks and we were encamped in Shelbyville. Now we were leaving for California on a train. This was November, 1942 through Needles, California.

The train would make many stops and the men would be left off to stretch their legs. Soldiers would be guarded so that none would go AWOL or desert into the towns. Our meals were on the train and were excellent. At some train stops, young boys would come up to the train and we would give them money and ask them to get some things at the town store. Neither the money nor the boys ever reappeared. Live and learn. The scenery of the landscape traveling west seemed so majestic, especially approaching California.

This was exciting – a land that always fascinated me when I was a boy – summer weather all year around – fruits and sunshine and we were there – but where – in the desert on to the beginning of desert warfare maneuvers. The Rockies glistened in sunlight and some still had snowcaps.

The train stopped in Needles and the soldiers climbed out onto half-tracks, tanks, and trucks to reach our area in the desert – Camp Ibis or Camp Young, California. Pyramid tents were raised and eight men to a tent were assigned.

All companies had there own area in alphabetical order in parallel lines with the company headquarters (C.O.) at the head.

Route 40 was a little ways off and this later on was found to be the way into the cities of southern California. This was the Mojave Desert – days were hot, sometimes over 120 degrees – on the hot sands and dropping down at night so many degrees that blankets were needed to keep warm. The excitement of being in California was soon forgotten – this was hot-cold sand and training. Many were the days patrols out on maneuvers were disoriented and the only possible way to get back 50 miles or so to camp was to locate the electric towers and follow them to a road and get our bearing back to camp. We were learning – map reading, compass, and dead reckoning procedures.

The companies would take pride in their area and landscape with stones and try to beautify their grounds. Each platoon tried their best to outdo each other and be the best they could be.

Sandstorms were many. Some of them were so thick you had to walk backwards to go forward because the sand would pepper our faces. Life was not as exciting. Sometimes we had cases of beer (Lucky Lager) that we bought from Needles or Blythe. We had forced marches with gas masks on. Some of the men passed out from the heat and were picked up by the first aid vehicles following to the rear of the column. We had many 25 mile hikes and forced marches with full field packs and equipment to try to complete in a certain amount of time – four or six hours – this was to build up our stamina to withstand and fight the enemy or retreat to a more defensible position. In our leisure time, there were many games, baseball, volleyball, races, poker, blackjack and craps. We had the best championship softball team in the armored infantry. Before entering the army I was a semi- pro baseball player. There were also passes to Las Vegas. I remember the Pioneer and the Frontier Casinos, but the Flamingo was not built yet.

The distances of hills in the desert seemed closer than they really were and they actually were miles away.

In the desert on maneuvers, some of the exercises were with live ammunition and artillery rounds would be shot over our heads as we advanced. Feeling cocky, on one exercise advancing through tumbleweed and cactus, I kept hollering, "Let's go one more time!" at the top of my voice. Not knowing that the company commander and the 1st Sgt. were watching our squad.

I'm sure of what they saw and heard, promoted me from a Private to a Corporal.

This type of training caused some casualties from artillery rounds falling short. Tanks would cross dry ditches and run over the foxholes occupied by our men. Whenever pitching the pup tents, we dug shallow trenches around them. In the desert you had to watch for Rattlesnakes and Gila Monsters. While encamped in the Texas panhandle, we were scared when an armadillo ran through our tent and startled us.

The best times of California and Nevada were the furloughs or passes into the cities especially, Los Angeles, the casino's of Las Vegas and the dinners and the shows. Mickey Dwyer and I went to L.A. many times and he had a way of attracting women. We always shared a room in the city and during one of our visits something really funny happened. A young lady knocked at my door and she said that Mickey sent her up to get some rest. I let her in and she promptly spread out on the bed and she stayed that way for ten minutes before leaving the room. When Mickey returned to the room he asked, "What happened?" I said, "Nothing!" Mickey said he sent her up to me to have some fun. I said, "Is that what she wanted?" We both had a good laugh. G.I.'s usually would return to camp broke, but it made no difference to the G.I. at camp. We had a place to stay and rations to eat. Water was trucked in from the water tanks in Blythe. Food would come in by trucks along with other supplies and ammunition. We had many different types of weapons and we were trained to fire them all, take them apart – clean them – put them back together. I made many new friends from different companies but many I would never see again as we were beginning to break up camp to go elsewhere – thinking we were being shipped out to combat – which some were, but we were sent to Texas to Camp Bowie.

At Camp Bowie, the 51st Infantry Regiment was broken down into battalions. Thus I was now in the 10th Armored Battalion. We went through obstacle courses again for our training. Texas was hot and humid especially on many foot marches. We went on maneuvers to Fort Hood for armored attacks and slept in the field. The drinking water was putrid so we usually drank beer or soda from the Post Exchange or from the towns of Ft Worth or Dallas. Brownwood was a dry county and the people were upset that alcohol beverages were brought in and they tried to stop it. General Wood would have none of that and said, if his men can fight for their country, they ought to be able to have a drink. That was that. Being a dry county, some of the soldiers would always find a way to obtain booze from other areas.

At the PX you could buy many things for less than the public would pay. When we received our pay, laundry bills and post exchange coupons were deducted. A soldier could set aside a certain amount for war bonds. I accumulated quite a bit. When you are fighting, attacking and taking the high ground, and also out in the desert, there are very few places to spend your money. I did alright in my army life between my winnings and my savings, and I saved $4500 that was later used to start my dry cleaning business.

In Dallas, Texas on a three day pass with my buddy, Mickey Dwyer, we would make the rounds of the bars. At one bar, I believed it was called the "Dungeon" or "The Pirate's Den", we became friendly with two young girls. This one girl, Edie Mae, stuck to me like glue. We spent more time in the room than in the bars. I had to surrender. I told Mickey, "Let's get out of here before she kills me!"

From Camp Bowie I received a furlough and went home for 10 days. What a relief! There was a newspaper story in Torrington about me returning to Fort Hood in Kileen Texas and that I had been in desert training in Indio, California. A Torrington lady called me and stated in conversation, how she grew up in Indio and Barstow. It was a pleasant call and this started a relationship. When I returned to camp, I received many letters from her that she was going West and would like to see me. A soldier should never say "No" to a lady. Before long we met in Temple, Texas. She was a beautiful lady of 35 years of age who was going through a divorce. We hit it off beautifully in room 606 in Temple, Texas. Night after night she would wait for me in the hotel lobby passing her time talking to the hotel guests. She was great company and a pleasant way to relieve the army pressures and duties. Many times I would just make it back for reveille. I would skip breakfast to get a little shuteye for 20 minutes before falling out for first call. I had some good times in Temple, Texas and on one of these nights coming back to camp, I did not know my company commander was also coming back from a furlough and he saw me but I did not see him. The next morning, he called me into the office, had me on the carpet and asked me what I was doing without a pass in town. I denied it and looked him straight in the eye. He kept asking and I still denied it telling him I had been in town other times but not last night. I know he didn't believe me but he must have liked my standing up to him. Thus I kept my Sgt.'s stripes because I would have been a private again. This affair ended with my ten day furlough to my home town of Torrington, Connecticut while she headed for California.

Being home on furlough was a very relaxing and an enjoyment of idleness. There was no reveille, no retreat, and no orders to obey. I had a great time and many parties.

At home, I met Phillip Cianciolo who was also on furlough and having met a couple of girls we knew, we made a date. I asked my brother Ray to lend me his DeSoto for the date. Looking for a place to park for a rendezvous off the beaten track, we became mired in mud on a dirt road. I had to call my friend, Bill Gleason, to winch us out with his wrecker. Bill, with a smile on his face, did not charge us a dime. It was a total disaster, romantically.

There was one unpleasant experience at home, when a woman and her daughter stopped me downtown and I expected a greeting. She berated me for not being overseas as her son who was in the National Guard and was in the islands, and she asked why I was home? Her daughter dragged the mother away before any more insults by her mother.

On the return trip to Camp Bowie Texas, on the train ride, I had to stand all the way to Chicago occasionally sitting on my duffle bag in the aisle. From Chicago to camp, I gave my seat to a young lady with a baby. The trains were loaded with soldiers.

After our training at Camp Bowie we went aboard a troop train to a port of debarkation that was Myles Standish in Massachusetts.

In the camp at Myles Standish, which was in the woods, we marked time for a few days before debarkation, so being off duty, I traveled into the city of Boston to be with my brother Mario. He had an apartment on Commonwealth Avenue in the Back Bay of Boston. He was very excited and surprised to see me after months of separation.

I spent a few days, from Saturday to Monday morning with him.

We went out Saturday and had dinner and the next day as we were walking along Commonwealth Avenue, we passed a drugstore that had a pay telephone and I decided to call Torrington to my parents. I was told not to tell where I was for security reasons – but I had to call my mother. She was ecstatic to hear my voice and for some reason – telepathy maybe – she knew I was with Mario as she explained she had a dream that on Saturday night I was with Mario.

She told the family the next morning, but they said to mother "It's only a dream."

I suppose if it wasn't for gasoline rationing, they would have made the trip to see me.

Somehow I managed to obtain a Christmas pass for three days.

The welcome with open arms will never be forgotten – relations, friends, and most of all my parents, brothers and sisters. My brother Fred came home from the Air Force.

The parting to go is so painful to my parents. I know it placed much stress on my mother, body and soul as the thought must have occurred to her that this could be the last time to be together.

Chapter V

England, We Are Coming

On December 28, 1943 we embarked on a ship called the Thomas Barry, a creaky old ship, named after a famous Navy officer. He probably was the founder of the American Navy during the American Revolution. As we sailed out of Boston Harbor, I could see men on the roof of the Charlestown Navy Yard waving us on. I know my brother Mario was there.

The ship rolled with each wave, creaking as she went and many soldiers were sea-sick.

We were passengers loaded in bunks to capacity – Thank God – with the whole convoy protected by destroyers and other naval ships, the crossing went well to a safe landing except for a mishap for two young soldiers washed overboard into the ocean by a sudden swell of a large wave. A destroyer was dispatched to go back for them, but they were never found. The Atlantic is cold and rough at this time of year.

On board, we would have exercises and drills, but on free time, games of chance were played, movies were shown, and we had some good and some bad conversations.

Oh, how we hoped that the war would be settled before we reached the battle zone.

We disembarked at the Firth of Wales. Trains were waiting to take us to Devizes where trucks transported us to the Nissen Huts (Quonset Huts).

Devizes was a small beautiful English town – thatched roof houses, little ponds, swans and ducks. We remained in Devizes a short time as the town was overloaded with troops. While we were in Devizes, we had many marches through their winding narrow streets until we were to be sent to Chippenham, some kilometers away.

The memories of Chippenham included – marches through the streets, exercises in field maneuvers, passes to Bristol, Bath, London, Manchester, Birmingham, and other places. The maneuvers continued on the moors of the southwestern part of England. These maneuvers were easier than those in America. Sometimes the boys would joke around and taunt each other. One day, riding the half-track, I said I was a sharpshooter, blowing my own horn. A comment was made that I could not hit the side of a barn. I took the ribbing, but it continued. The taunting finally raised my temper. I said, "I'll show you, see that bevy of quail over their, just watch!" The quail were about a hundred yards away. I raised my M-1 Garand rifle and pulled off a shot and lo and behold, I not only blew apart a quail, but killed another on a ricochet. All ribbing subsided and we all had a laugh. This happened again with my "A" Co. at the end of the war.

While encamped, guards were posted in the mess hall to make sure that the G.I.'s ate everything on their plates and not waste food. This jingle comes to mind:

When reaching the line, don't load your plate.
Come back for seconds, you won't be late.
So help yourself and make your meal a delight.
To see you happy is a pleasant sight.
Don't waste a bit and clean up your plate.
Come back for seconds, you won't be late.

I intended, as long as I was in England, to see all I could, like the Bristol Philharmonic Orchestra, London's Big Ben, 10 Downey St. – the Prime Minister's residence, Hyde Park, Trafalgar Square, Madame Tussaud's Wax Museum, Westminster Abbey, St. Paul's Cathedral, Soho, Whitehall and Liverpool Stations on the underground (subway). The underground was so deep that it was a very safe air raid shelter where many people slept at night because of nightly air raids. London and many places in England had balloon barrages. Balloons attached to long cables high into the air, were used so that the enemy aircraft could not do low level bombing and strafing. The joke about the balloons was if there were no balloons England would sink into the sea from the mass of material and manpower weight on the island. The nights were blackouts – shades down, windows closed, no outside lights, no fires, except the ones caused by bombing.

People would sometimes be oblivious to the bombing and go about whatever they were doing. I was dining with Nurse Lt. Irene Calantuno in a fashionable upstairs restaurant and we, along with other diners continued to dine while the bombs were falling. Many were the stares at a Sergeant walking, then dining, with a Lieutenant.

In Chippenham we'd go into town for fish and chips (at a cost of one shilling six Pence about .35 cents). They would rap them in newspaper and we ate them at the barracks. Also at other stores and pubs we practically bought all their food – breads, cakes, etc. Soon some of the people were annoyed as the supply was diminishing for them. Also, the English soldiers were envious and annoyed at the Americans for making it difficult for female company because we had more money to spend than the English and they said that we were overpaid, over-sexed and over here.

At times it was very lonely for the American soldier. To relieve some of the boredom – we'd get together with the English WRAF.

A dance would be scheduled for a Saturday night at a large building in our barracks area. The pairing of the English girls and the American G.I.'s were done by numbers that matched each other. It was fun. Some were paired with tall, others with short – switching could be made if necessary. One particular night after the pairing, some of the G.I.'s would disappear for awhile and then return. This was happening all night. The English girls couldn't understand why.

Tech. Sgt. Eugene W. Luciano

Camp Croft, S.C. The new recruits.

Camp Croft, S.C.

Fort Devens, Mass. 1941.

October 1941. 33rd Training Battalion, Camp Croft, S.C.
Front row: Rudy Hirchak, Pat Quinn, Art Pergola,
Art Compito. Phil Cianciola, Gene Luciano.
Standing: Frostberg, Armond Polutro.

The visit, August 1941.

Pine Camp.

Furlough
January 1945.

Steel
Helmet
Rookie

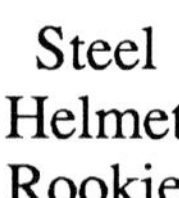

Our Barracks.

Softball Champs 1943. Mgr. Adrien Tessier.

Top Row: Stickford, Silas, Braden, Montello, Vail.
Second row: Kupros, Osmanski, Painter.
Front: Watts, Grbovac, Sacco, Luciano.

Art and Gene. Home.

Desert inspection.

Noel and me, England.

Wilkens, me, Keane, England.

Top: Salber, Oliver, Knight, Bob Wall, Gene.

Goldbricking.

Desert Sagebrush.

Gene, Harry Knight.

The family: Ray, Antoinette, Mom, Pop, Enes. Rear: Fred, John, me, (Mario) missing.

Art Compito,
my cousin.

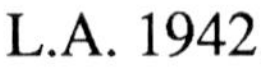

L.A. 1942.

Montell cutting Genes hair.

Sand storm, California.

Fratercangelo,
Gene,
Carmen Basso.

Art Compito,
Gene,
Tony Penzone.

It seems that on this particular evening the meal gave everyone in the company dysentery.

The latrine was an open long lean-to shed with a long bench with holes with pails beneath to catch the waste – and were they ever overflowing! Pity the men with horse and wagon, unloading the pails into their large horse drawn tank and bringing it to the sewerage plant every morning.

Of course some of the boys had to go into the fields to relieve themselves as there was no room on the toilet seats.

The young WRAF that I drew came from a very influential London family. We dated a few times and we seemed to hit it off in a very friendly manner. The last date was never fulfilled because of restriction of everyone to barracks. We were supposed to meet at the railroad station the evening of the surprise restriction. We were placed on military alert and that night the sky was loaded with bombers in formation on a massive aerial strike onto the continent, especially Germany. This was about a month before the invasion.

I never saw her again as we were sent down to guard the southern shore of England around Torquay and Plymouth so the Navy could go about their preparation and exercises for the storming of the French beaches.

The American G.I. had USO clubs to go have some fun, also English clubs where WRAF girls, the Land Army girls would go. Some of our Americans met their English wives here.

One of the young English service girls I felt sorry for was from the city of Coventry, the city that was devastated by the night raid of enemy bombers. It was rumored that Prime Minister Churchill knew of the upcoming bombing by the German Luftwaffe but he could not alert or warn the citizens of Coventry because he did not want to tip off the Germans that their code had been broken. We had a few dates together in London where we did the town. She spent the night at women's service personal lodging while I spent a few shillings at a room I rented on the third floor. We liked to do and see the same historical things, and then back to camp.

Having a high IQ along with a Sgt. Ray and an assigned officer, Major Abraham Baum (Author of the book, "Raid", about the Hammelburg Mission to rescue Gen. Patton's son-in-law, Colonel John Waters), I was selected to attend a secret assignment for learning secret codes through all letters (that were to be screened at Headquarters) whenever I sent them home. In those letters would be information by code of what was going on. Of course this would be used if I was taken as a prisoner of war. God forbid, I did not have to use the code. In hindsight, I know why I was used on many patrols to gather information and make contact between our platoons. I chose my birthday for my code number (04/20/16). Although many years have passed, I still remember a few code details. The result of subtracting a number from the mentioning of a day within the body of the letter, such as Christmas, like "1225" would signify the code. The individual code digits were used to count-out words to construct a short message. One specific word to indicate the start of spelling, for example, was the word "and".

I was graded by some staff members in E.T.O. Headquarters so I believe. She said to try to not make it too simple because it was somewhat stilted. My Company Commander, while I was at this training in England, asked me what was going on. He had orders to release me temporarily. Since I was sworn to secrecy, I told him, "Sorry sir, I am not at liberty to divulge any information as this has nothing to do with the operations of this platoon." He was satisfied. Maybe he knew and was testing me. Thus, I had a little relief from drilling and classes.

Before breaking up camp in Chippenham, the company was ordered to fall out at the flagpole on the Drill Grounds for an important briefing before entering combat. Officers gave specific details of what to expect in the days ahead, explaining the Normandy situation. I think the battalion medical officer said, "Some of you will not return and will buy the farm." Orders were given for soldiers to prepare their last simple will and power of attorney. Finally leading us in prayer, the unit was dismissed. I was chosen and assigned to write and witness each simple will and power of attorney.

Years later, a good friend, Anthony Penzone trying to locate me for years, stumbled on this document and found my address. He turned out to be a successful business man running the Florentine Restaurant on Broad St. in Columbus, Ohio. We corresponded. When we were out there on a 4th Arm'd Assn. Convention, we dined at his restaurant. When I asked for Tony, his son told me his father had died recently. The son treated us very well.

Tony was an excellent cook in civilian life. The mess sergeant at times, let Tony cook an Italian meal. The dinner was well received by the whole company. Tony and I travelled to L.A. many times. On April 19,1943, on the eve of my 27th birthday we celebrated at the World famous Biltmore Hotel with two lady friends.

Now the time had come – about four (4) years of training. We were ready. On July 9, 1944 we left our barracks for the shores of the southern part of England to embark up on ships to cross the English Channel. Goodbye England – Hello France!

Chapter VI

Goodbye England, Hello France

As our LCI's and LCT's approached the Utah beach, the debris was floating with G.I. cans, miscellaneous equipment and an occasional body bobbing in the water.

Our landing had to be delayed until the tide went out and the waters receded from the ships. After some time the ship's gate was unlatched and the half-tracks loaded with the men and equipment set upon the beach. The sight of many of our dead and wounded and the German prisoners waiting to be sent to prisoners of war enclosures was the realization of the dangers that laid ahead. "This wasn't maneuvers, this was the real thing and what in the hell am I doing here?" Over in the distance an enemy observation plane was seen twirling in rapid descent – shot down by land based gunners.

The time was mid afternoon on July 13, 1944. The battalion, having landed, went to the left, heading in the wrong direction, perhaps into the Canadian or English section or towards the enemy. Only when someone alerted the battalion about the mistake, and made the necessary change to move to our bivouac area which was near St. Mere Eglise and northeast of Perriers.

It seemed so peaceful even though shellfire could be heard in the distance. After bivouac, with our vehicles around the perimeter of the field, guards were posted and we rested for the night. In the night, shells must have fallen in our area as shell holes were visible, but there were no casualties. One soldier getting into his foxhole, accidently shot himself and had to be evacuated.

The next day, many French people and especially young boys were very curious to talk to us and were elated to see our equipment and ask questions until the order was to cease and desist with information to not jeopardize our position. It began to rain and it continued all day long. As time passed, the troops were restless and becoming impatient standing around for three days with very little activity. Many of us , to get out of the rain, would go to the edge of the field and stand under the trees. Remembering back to that time – my friend Mickey Dwyer and others got the bright idea that since we were out of sight, now was the time to unload and bury all of our impregnated clothing at the base of the trees. Many things were impregnated against the affects of water, etc. and perhaps a gas attack.

About the fourth day some "90-day wonder" (a new 2nd Lieutenant) had us all in a skirmish line advancing, slowing, and sticking our bayonets very carefully into the ground. We were to clear the field of possible mines. Of course, the men had already walked over the area on the previous days so it seemed so foolish to be checking it now. All this time, we were anxious to get on the move. The front lines were only a few miles ahead and the beachhead was a very small area. Troops were being landed continually and sooner than later we would have to enlarge the area to accommodate all the equipment being put ashore. One important detail is that the air cover and our air support of the area protected men and equipment from enemy counterattacks trying to push our backs to the sea.

This is not how my impressions of France had appeared to me in my youth.

On the day of July 17, 1944, we relieved an infantry division in the line. It was either the 4th Infantry or 29th Infantry Division. This is when I saw my first dead German soldier. He was laying beneath a large tree, bloated and seemed green to me. I notified my superiors, but they said the graves registration personnel would take care of all casualties. Then as we were ready to take our position in the line, a shot caught a lieutenant right in the middle of his forehead. He never knew what hit him.

This was at Periers, Raids and La Maugerie. We lost some of our men and suffered casualties. We helped evacuate a couple of boys from their front positions who were wounded and placed them in a ditch a hundred yards or so back. We gave them first aid and tried to stem their chest wounds and also sprinkled sulfa on the injuries. They were mortally wounded and one kept calling his mother, "Ma, Ma". As we were trying to ease his pain and dress the wounds some officer whom I did not know, told us to leave him alone and get back up on the line. We were still under fire, but the officer acted as if we were still on maneuvers.

I was scared but there was no place to go but back to the fire fight behind the stone wall. At nightfall, all turned quiet except the brbr-brbr-brbr-brbr of the burp gun to keep us awake. Being scared is not unusual. Good leaders hide their fears and act bravely when they are with their men on any mission or patrol to instill confidence to the men in the leader's ability. Any man in combat who claims he is not frightened or scared is not truthful. A brave soldier is also a scared soldier. The only soldiers, not running scared, are dead ones. Even though I came from a religious family, also serving the church as an altar boy, I became very lax in religion. How quick I found it in the foxholes, especially at Arracourt when we were under attack. There's an old saying, "There are no atheists in foxholes." How well I know. Thank God for our chaplains.

Some other emotions are home sickness, loneliness, and sadness. When hearing sentimental songs such as "You'll Never Know", sung by a 27 year old Frank Sinatra would give one a romantic and longing feeling and also "White Christmas", sung by crooner Bing Crosby would bring back wonderful memories of home. Suddenly, you are saddened and wistful. A soldier is not afraid to shed a tear or cry on the loss of a buddy on the battlefield. Happiness is shown by soldiers when a mission is successful and completed. These are some of the many emotions a soldier experiences.

In the night time, Captain Leighton called me to take a squad and keep contact with the companies of the battalion, on a patrol because the radios were silenced. I stooped and crawled with the squad using a password to make contact till early morning. The early morning hours were very hazardous and as we went along the road, mortar shells would almost have us zeroed in. The Germans had all the ranges for mortar fire already setup, especially at the hedgerows. As we stopped and then moved about fifty feet, one could hear the mortar shells and see where they landed, where we had been just moments earlier. That happened a few times and then it stopped because some of our guns in the rear were firing at their positions and they pulled back.

There could have been a spotter, back of our lines, when we were on patrol telling our position for those mortar shots – possibly French. Later on Sgt. Tessier said he shot a sniper out of a tree.

Company "C" was pulled out of this line. I lost Pvt. Corcoran in action in this skirmish and Pvt. Holmes was with him when he got shot. When I peered over the hedgerows, I fell back immediately because of enemy fire. I jarred my helmet into the bridge of my nose causing injury. This was our baptism of fire.

The hedgerows were created by many years of Norman and French farmers clearing the debris and resulting undergrowth which formed borders for the fields. This formed a bank of hedgerows, four to five feet thick and high.

On the 19th of July, we heard through rumors that efforts were being made so that the war would soon be over. There was joy everywhere. It never happened. This must have been the attempt on Hitler's life.

This same day we were sent on a mission led by Lt. Robberts to the right of where we were holding the line with "A" Co. We attacked and laid all kinds of firepower as we advanced only to later realize we were firing on some of our own engineers to the right flank. Being "green" troops, we were using-up our ammunition in rapid-fire, not even knowing what we were firing at. The German fire was more deliberate with mortar and sporadic bursts of their guns. No damage was done as somehow the situation corrected itself and we attacked and drove straight forward advancing perhaps 100 yds. or so until Captain Leighton fell mortally wounded. The attack was broken off and the line held. At nightfall Lt. Spencer and Sgt. Tessier went out to get the Captain under cover of darkness. He was still alive but died soon after so they said. For the next few days, there was an exchange of artillery and gunfire, but very little advancement.

The hedgerows were a stumbling block to us as the Germans had them all zeroed in. For the next ten days we fought at a standstill. We did not lose any territory or gain very much. A way had to be found to use our motorized equipment and when a soldier came up with the steel wedge welded to the bulldozer to cut through the 4 foot thick hedgerows so that the tanks, half-tracks, and guns could move through, and we could attack and use the training we learned in the Mojave Desert in California. Some of the material used to make these wedges of steel came from obstacles in the water and the beaches where their purpose was to prevent us from invading France.

Chapter VII

Breakout and Breakthrough

The breakout of the Normandy Beach area perimeter, the greatest air power that ever was assembled flew over the front lines and the sky was almost cut off from sunlight. The ground shook and trembled as the bombs fell ahead of our front line with some falling short and killing our own boys including Gen. McNair. The smoke from our own bombs drifting toward our lines caused the pilots to bomb short. I didn't know what was happening. The artillery laid down a heavy barrage that must have stunned the German-held territory. We went through the opening and were free to maneuver and there were many dead and wounded enemy and also many prisoners were being marched to the rear to a prisoner of war camp. Much enemy equipment was lost. Riding through St. Lo, the debris from the bombed buildings had to be bulldozed to make passage through St. Lo guided through with Military Police. We raced and quickly captured Coutances, on July 28. Gen. Patton (Blood and Guts!") now took over and the Third Army was in action. One could not believe the sights of picturesque villages being ruined by warfare. One beautiful place offshore was Mont St. Michel. The 8th Fighter Command plus other bombers along with our relentless pursuit smashed many retreating columns, one of which had the German payroll for their army. These were horse drawn vehicles along with motorized vehicles. The money was everywhere. The G.I.'s were scooping it up and filling up their seat covers in the half-tracks and other vehicles. On July 30 orders came down from Command Headquarters to move out at 6 AM with "C" Company leading the 10th Arm'd Infantry Battalion going through the towns of La Pelletierie, La Mt. Raintree, Le Chailloast, and Coutances.

The people were coming out to greet us with flowers, wine and kisses. One Frenchman was very upset because many houses were hit by heavy fire but when the tanker threw him hands full of Francs, he went wild with happiness. Most of us thought the money had no value because the Germans had it. How wrong we were! We bivouacked at Coutances and we could hear enemy vehicles moving out in retreat.

The breakthrough, called "Cobra" was now into the open. This was a brilliant plan devised by Gen. Omar Bradley. There were scenes of many dead and demoralized German soldiers. Many cows were killed and bloated. Houses and buildings were demolished. There was mud all over and the stench of dead animals and decaying flesh, rained soaked clothes, and shoes was an appalling, stinking sight. High in a tree, stuck between the branches,was a cow. There were many crater holes from the bombing. The front was very fluid. It was very risky because we were making a fast attack into enemy lines and there was the possibility of being cutoff from our lines of supplies. We were on the outskirts of Avranches, July 31. We were stopped momentarily, but pushed right through and captured more prisoners and equipment and more French people came out with wine, flowers and kisses happily shouting, clapping, applauding and very jubilant after four years of German occupation. General John Wood, our division commander, came up and sized up the situation and must have decided to keep going. The column moved hastily on Aug. 2 towards Rennes. On the outskirts we met token resistance on the way and fought our way into the city. In this engagement we lost our battalion commander, Col. Kilpatrick who was badly wounded. The Germans made another counter-attack on our left flank but were stopped by artillery and from the 8th Air Force smashing their column to bits. They retreated in droves. After crossing a canal into the city we assembled in a sunken garden so it seemed. Enemy tanks were burning in the city.

Later we bivouacked outside the city and for the first time we received the "10 in 1" rations. I was sent out to secure the Ducey Dams from sabotage (if the dams were bombed, it would have flooded the area and delayed our advancement). On the way some noises were heard and my platoon with Manzitto, Slavik, Holmes, Johnson, Salber, Knight, Slater, and Rossing cut through some tall grass and underbrush hacking with our bayonets and machetes. There was no resistance. The squad spent the night in the woods on the outpost. The only enemy was "Midnight Charlie" flying over the area.

We were now in the Brittany area heading south toward Bain de Bretaine while other columns were heading towards Brest, so we could have a seaport. As we advanced, infantry units were mopping-up the enemy soldiers to our rear.

My duty was to set up an outpost about five miles from the company which was accomplished.

At a crossroad, I set up a 30 cal. water cooled machine gun along with the half-track concealed in the bushes. Everything was quiet this day except for a girl riding down the road on a bicycle. She was stopped, searched and let go on her way. In the morning we joined the company at their bivouac area. We were ordered to head south towards the Channel ports of St. Nazaire, Lorient, Nantes and Vannes. The submarine pens of the Wolfpack were there in concrete bunkers. The area was well fortified so we sealed off the area till the end of the war, bottling up many of the enemy. This containment was turned over to the VIII Corps of General Middleton's 6th Arm'd Division.

Chapter VIII

Tears For Mickey

Early one morning in an engagement on Aug. 5, 1944 in Brittany, we attacked a German position. Sgt. Dwyer and his squad went straight down the road with Pvt. Groom manning the half-track's 50 cal. machine gun. My squad was off to the left cutting through tall grass and underbrush with our bayonets and machetes until we came up to a hedgerow. As I peered over the hedgerow to recointre the area, a shot whistled by my head stopping our advance. Sgt. Dwyer wasn't having any luck on his side either and had to withdraw leaving Lt. Robbert's jeep and equipment behind. On withdrawing, Pvt. Groom, manning the half-track and shooting the 50 cal. machine gun was mortally wounded and died on the battlefield. We were stalemated and were forced to withdraw to our outpost and we lost our jeep with Lt. Robberts' equipment. In the distance, as we were withdrawing, I could see some Germans getting out of their foxholes. Later that night, patrolling on the hillside and as it was very dark, I thought as I passed a clump of bushes I heard a rustling and muffled sound. There was no way I was going to start a fight in darkness. Trying to recover our jeep the next day resulted in the loss of S/Sgt. Mickey Dwyer, my buddy in the states. A very great loss for me. Early in the morning Lt. Robberts with Sgt. Mickey Dwyer and his squad moved to try to get the belongings out of the jeep that was left behind. It was a failure. Sgt. Dwyer was killed. Our platoon was notified when we were on outpost by Lt. Robberts and for the first time tears streamed down my face as Mickey was one of my dear friends. In the states, we would go out together. He had a way with the opposite sex and always could find company. One day in Nashville, he got me a date with his girl friend's sister. His date was a doll, my date was average. I rented a car from an agency at about 12 noon and returned it at 12:30 AM. The rental agent must have been confused because he only charged for one hour. We had a wonderful time visiting all the landmarks of Nashville. For a time, when we were in California for desert maneuvers, we wrote to them but they passed into history. Sometimes I wondered where and what became of them, but then again so many episodes happened in the life of a soldier that all is left behind in memories. Now Mickey Dwyer was gone and all of a sudden I became a hardened soldier and all my hate for the enemy was instilled in me. I originally entered this army just to do my time and go home, but now it was to do my part for the loss of my friend.

The outpost was scary. Soldiers always imagine hearing noises. Sometimes my own ears ringing would startle me causing me to be more alert. In those early days we slept very little. The night was noisy because of sporadic machine gun fire, and the Germans had patrols out traveling and scouting around the area. Early in the morning, when the sun hadn't yet risen, the German patrol crossed the road 100 yds. to our front. An alert private opened fire and the patrol dispersed only to set up a machine gun and rake our area with machine gun fire and then withdrew. We had no casualties. After checking the area to our front, there laying dead in a ditch, was a strong German soldier. A couple of hours later, coming to our outpost was a white flag leading the German patrol along with the Germans who stopped our attack the day before and surrendered. Thus our mission was accomplished. How fortunate for them. The war was over. Then we found out we had been using the same well for water and it was fortunate we never met there. After the German patrol surrendered to us, we were relieved by an infantry outfit and we regrouped in an apple orchard to get cleaned, shaved and washed and to replenish supplies and ammunition. We wrote letters and spoke of different experiences. General John Wood wanted to head for Paris before going south to Lorient and attack to the east but was overruled by General Patton. Who knows if the war would have ended sooner?

There were times when during blackout columns would pass each other at night and everyone being quiet, neither column knew they were passing by each other going the other way. I know once it was German because we learned later that they bivouacked near us for the night. Who knows if the war would have ended sooner?

There were also times when there was a lull in fighting and we were not advancing and if there was an opportunity to pause in a vineyard or under a fruit tree. My driver, Don Durkes, would do so. I can remember picking off plums while standing up in our half-track.

The damage that armored vehicles caused to farms, vineyards and trees, were no comparison to the destruction of houses, buildings, and towns smashed into ruins.

We knew we were running ahead so quickly that we did not have maps of the terrain, we were beyond the latest ones. I wouldn't be surprised if Hdqs. were only going by road signs or auto maps.

When we were moving on to an objective, the vehicles kept 50 yds. apart and under 30 kilometers per hour during daylight hours; but in night blackout driving they would close-in trying to keep the vehicle ahead in contact, perhaps by a small reflection or from moonlight. Traveling in convoys, there were always guides to direct the column at crossroads or in darkness. An M.P. or one of our combat soldiers would drop off to act as a guide. The guide would be picked up by the last vehicle in the column. The standing half-track or tank commanders were the eyes of the driver to keep him on his course. The vehicles were directed by commands, "a little right, a little left or straight ahead". A standing commander was a good target for snipers. I know I heard an occasional shot hit the half-track and also zip past me as we advanced.

The orders were now to head for Lorient on the southern coast. This was about August 10th, 1944. We traveled the distance with very little resistance. German prisoners were marching back in rows with hands on top of their heads. Many lost their will to fight from the heavy bombing and strafing of our Air Force and Artillery. They were very shakened and knew the war was over for them. We went into a bivouac area in Lorient and Vannes. I remember I could see the ocean at Vannes. Continuing our advance to the enemy submarine lairs at St Nazaire, a heavily fortified area, we encircled the area and isolated the enemy and turned the defense over to the 6th Arm'd Division, I believe. This action neutralized this opposition for the duration of the war. During bivouac, we had an opportunity to get our equipment, guns, and ourselves cleaned up. Later our orders were to head back, I believe to Bain de Bretagne and make an advance towards Orleans. A German Army on the south side of the Loire River surrendered. They were disarmed and sent to a prisoner of war enclosure.

CHAPTER IX

ORLEANS AND BEYOND

We turned east, north of the Loire River heading towards Orleans. This was the time when much of the German army could have been caught, but they escaped with men and equipment, through the Falaise Gap, because Gen. Montgomery did not move fast enough from the north to close the gap. General Montgomery was a very cautious general compared to General Patton's daring and guts, of course very reckless with our blood.

Many technical mistakes lengthened the duration of the war, such as Montgomery's blunders and his insistence to Gen. Dwight Eisenhower for all of the supplies (especially petroleum) which were also needed by Patton's Third Army. The result of this action brought the Third Army's drive to a standstill and thus, the German armies had time to bolster their defenses and reorganize against the Fourth Armored Division and the rest of the Third Army.

When Gen. John S. Wood's 4th Armored Division turned east towards Orleans, there were many small engagements and many towns were liberated. Since there was a thunderstorm and lightening, we waited and dug foxholes outside the city. In the distance many large fires in the city of Orleans could be seen. The evacuating Germans in their haste, were burning everything to keep the equipment and supplies from being captured and used against them. We traveled through the airfield that was mined – single file and did not lose anyone or any vehicle. We took the city after a firefight and captured many prisoners.

The people of Orleans were jubilant and greeted us as Liberators – saying, "The Boche are kaput!" and believing the war would soon be over. Of course some of the sympathizers would say, "You're winning now, but wait."

Some who fraternized with the enemy were mauled. Girls were abused and their heads were shaved. The French were rounding up their collaborators, stripping them naked and putting them on display in the town square. The women who entertained Germans with their favors were exposed and shamed. The resistance of the French people became very apparent. The Free French Forces (FFI) were now very active and helpful. They were making raids into the German rear areas.

There were times when we were strafed by enemy aircraft and also mistakenly fired upon by our own fighter pilots. A system was devised of marking our columns so that we would change our panel colors each day to foil the enemy's attempts to use our colors to protect themselves from attack by American aircraft. The panels had to be out immediately or we would sometimes be strafed. The panels were four by eight feet colored "canvas". The color of the panel would be changed daily so that our aircraft would know that we were friendly forces. This was a protection so that the enemy would not know the color we used for that day.

Mistakes were made with careless handling of guns. I can remember at Avranches during a lull in the fighting as I was resting against a rail post, the post was shattered by a tanker's gun as he hit the trigger accidently as the vehicles were halted in the middle of the road. I guess God was with me!

Also during a night attack in September, 1944 near the Moselle River, our one tank fired upon us and drove us into a farmhouse's cellar. We all shouted, scared and angry, at the tanker, "We are Yanks!" The firing suddenly stopped.

Leaving Orleans about August 21 1944, we traveled east into Sens and a fire fight. We arrived so swiftly that we caught the Germans unprepared and by surprise. Some of the enemy were walking in the town.

At Sens a warehouse was captured and it supplied enough cognac for the whole column and cases were mounted on most vehicles along with seat covers full with French francs from the German payroll.

On many roads, the trees were cut halfway to be dropped across the roads to stop our advance. Our movement caught them by surprise and they did not have time to complete their mission. Also, their heavy guns were abandoned.

Our next objective was the city of Troyes where the Germans made a strong defense. We bivouacked outside the city and at dawn's first light drove down from the top of the hill in a desert formation of armored vehicles spread out with the infantry advancing in marching fire as the heavy guns blasted the town. We had many casualties and Major Arthur West who led the attack, was badly wounded. Troyes was a very important objective for our advance to the east because it was a German strong point.

Moving on – night or day – daylight or black-out to St. Dizier, St. Genevieve, Commercy, with small fire fights on to each objective. The many "firing" techniques are: marching fire, is troops advancing, shooting straight ahead and is usually fired from the hip while advancing; in a defensive position, crossfiring with the right side shooting left across the field and the left side shooting right creating a blanket on the field of fire; mortar and artillery firing usually used bracketing and searching fire, shooting one long and one short at the target and then dividing the coordinates, hitting the target; firing for effect was to keep the enemy pinned down.

At Commercy, we took the high ground and could view the whole area to our front. We were soon to meet up with our 7th Army from the south. On that high mountain top, I set up an outpost on the slope overlooking the valley. In the distance, a German Infantry unit was marching towards the high ground, but retreated when they saw the situation. Then all hell broke loose. We were hit and strafed by the Luftwaffe. The men were dug into foxholes as I scrambled up the mountain and I found a very small depression between two rocks and fitted my small frame of

135 lbs. into this protection. The strafing caused a trail of bullet splatters to strike the ground causing some casualties. Close by me, a buddy, Pfc. Hofferer was killed. Our P-47 planes came a little too late.

It seems there was always streams and rivers to cross especially the same river with all its bends such as the Moselle, Meuse, and others. Into a sortie in what I believe was the town of St. Genevieve, I led a platoon into the village as the enemy was moving back on the horizon and I could see enemy vehicles pulling back. I setup coverage on one side of the road and Sgt. Keane, the other side along with Sgt. Noel. No sooner we were in position, a sidecar with two Germans came down the road, and Sgt.. Keane's men opened up and knocked them into a ditch. Some French came and took their equipment and watches as they were mortally wounded.

Word was brought up that the enemy was counterattacking so we withdrew a few miles to the rear so we would not be cutoff from the rest of our unit.

The counterattack did not materialize. The drive east continued. The objective was the capture of Nancy and to take Metz. In the capture of Nancy, the 4th Arm'd Division with CCA and CCB drove through the German lines with one combat command on the north and the other on the south side of the city with CCR in reserve. Driving deep into the German lines beyond the city, before completing the encirclement, many Germans evacuated the city. Some Germans escaped the entrapment, but many were captured as infantry troops mopped up the area. General Patton later set up his 3rd Army headquarters in Nancy. The 3rd Army was nicknamed "Lucky". If the supplies of gas and ammunition was not diverted from the 3rd Army to General Montgomery's plan in the north, I believe the war would have been over by Christmas. The delay of two weeks or so caused stiff resistance. The 4th Arm'd Division, having to withdraw, had to shorten our defensive position. Crossing a bridge over a small stream, shells were hitting on both sides of the bridge as the vehicles and men retreated to higher ground and dug in. I believe it was hill 265. We were being heavily shelled as they were attacking our position. We took many casualties. The diverting of the supplies really gave the Germans an advantage. The quick actions of our tanks, especially the 37th Tank Battalion and the 704th Tank Destroyers, saved the day. The tanks and M-18 Tank Destroyers fought the greatest tank battles of warfare ever. Enemy tanks, our tanks and tank destroyers, some in flames, were jockeying for advantageous positions. When the Germans fled the tank battle, out on that ground, there was an abundant mess of smashed and flaming vehicles. Though we lost a lot of equipment, we stopped their counterattack. I believe it was one of the greatest tank battle victories of the war. Later we took a defensive position on the outskirts and set our half-tracks in a line to the rear of our foxholes. If the Germans were successful in this drive to prevent our link-up with General Patch's 7th Army, they could have driven west and caused a lot of damage disrupting our timetable. The armor they used in the Battle of the Bulge could have been used as a wedge between the 7th and 3rd Armies. Who knows if they could have made a drive west into our rear lines?

The Moselle River was to be crossed at the Pont of Moussan and drive towards Chateau-Salins. The objective of the crossing was hotly contested before the enemy retreated on our drive to Chateau-Salins. The enemy hid snipers in haystacks and in barns. They were eliminated by tracer fire setting them ablaze. Another city was taken! The Combat Commands of the 4th Armored Division now turned south heading for Luneville where the enemy was counterattacking. Our mission was to close the gap between the Third Army and the Seventh Army under General Patch.

Now we received orders to turn in the German payroll we captured in Normandy. We were told to hand in all that we had. Many soldiers complied, except those who sent money home through quartermasters. I often wonder about the rumors that officers were sending money home by the thousands. When it was originally divided, each G.I. received $300 in French francs.

Chapter X

A Frenchman's Good Deed

Combat Commands "A" and "B" of the 4th Armored Division advanced northwest of the city holding C.C.R. in reserve on the outskirts. The German counterattack was coming from the northeast. The advance was stalled by the 4th Armored Division when the C.C. Reserve was called. Neither of the combatants had any advantage. It was a stalemate in the action, even though shells were falling in our rear areas. In late afternoon one of our tanks attempted to smash into their defense and was prevented by anti-tank fire, killing the crew. All was at a standstill. A Frenchman approached me and explained how Germans were covering a side road that ran beyond his house. He offered to let us into the backyard of his house which was about 200 yds. down the road behind the opponents.

Moving swiftly and cautiously, we rushed the rear of the house to the rear of the enemy's position. They were well camouflaged facing up the street with their backs towards us. Lt. Wilson had his pistol ready to fire. The squad had their guns at the ready, but before the order was given to fire, for some unknown reason I shouted, "Hands, Hoch!" To my surprise a whole enemy platoon turned and raised their hands. I commanded half of the squad to go to the side road and bring them out as our guns would cover them until they got out to the road. The reason being there was a high fence between the backyard and the enemy's position. We disarmed and sent them back to the rear. Now, the 4th Armored Division had to move on and turn the line over to other army units. For this action, Lt. Wilson said he would recommend the Silver Star for me and the men. The Silver Star recommendation was never written because Lt. Wilson was killed. It didn't matter to me at that time. My only thought was staying alive with my men.

In the early morning hours, at our new position, shells were falling in our bivouac area. The outfit decided to move forward. As the column began to move, the first three light tanks were knocked out. The armored infantry with tank support neutralized the enemy position but not before a direct hit killed our Lt. Wilson and our runner, Pfc. Long. The armored column being shelled, fought to withdraw to a more defensive position. In order to do so, the column was fighting a "hit and run" attack to withdraw to higher ground. We had to cross a bridge as the shells were falling on each side of it as the Germans were trying to stem our falling back to higher ground. The enemy attacked us fiercely with tanks and artillery until we reached higher ground. The enemy guns were falling continuously on our position, but now we were dug in. We lost some men including Sgt. Nelson. To reach this position, we traveled in desert formation at high

Pollutro
and me.

Watch is
waiting
the Battle.

Off to POW Cage Duty.

A Company 10th.

Lt. Miller, Czechkoslovakia.

Me.

Markleuten.

Markleuten Schoolhouse. Commandeered Billets.

Sgt. Plourde. Sussice, Czech.

Big shot Sgt.

Markleuten, Germany.

Dreaming of home.

Sgt. Kennedy.

Carmen Basso.

Combat Soldier Chemnitz, Germany.

Sgt. Michalek.

Near Chemnitz, Germany.

Bristol, England.

May 29, 1945

Dear Mom & Dad,

Tonight I sat along the banks of the Blue Danube watching the German children rowing their boats across the swift current of the river with an occasional American soldier as a passenger. The German girls would wave from the opposite bank but we cannot fraternize with them. It is very hard not to speak to them but we cannot afford to lose what we have won.

After looking at the blue waters for a spell, it seems that the opposite banks and the outlying hills are moving upstream. The river at this point in Kelheim is approximately 200 yds wide but as it winds on its merry way the river seems to widen out considerably. This is a very romantic land for beautiful scenery especially in this part of Germany where

Letter home (page 1).

2)

many mountains and mountain ranges are located. These mountains at this time of the year are green because of many trees.

Yesterday on our road march through Czechoslovakia into Germany, I saw many German soldiers loaded with packs on their way home and here am I waiting with my 101 points for my turn to be shipped home and finally discharged from the armed Forces of the U S army. It is funny to notice the change of people, the attitude, and customs of the German People to the Czech People. When we first left Germany the people could only stare as if to pinch themselves to see if this were true and the German Army defeated. These faces could never believe that America had so much equipment and good fighting men; but, now coming back into Germany, the people would like to greet in some way but they know of

Letter home (page 2).

3)

we cannot fraternize with them so they do all the work they can in their fields. Many are the women that do this work. They are a hard working lot. Coming into Czechoslovakia, the people went crazy trying to do things for us, trying to shake our hands, giving us flower and food. They were a happy lot but after being in about Pole for a couple of weeks, the people seem to get greedy and want many things from us but I guess that is natural because we have many small items they don't have. Going out of Czechoslovakia, some people watch, some people worked but it wasn't anything compared to our reception when we first hit their country. The same way with the French people.

Right now we are occupation forces at this place. It was a former wool factory. The town of Kelheim has a population of approximately 6,500 people and most of the people work

Letter home (page 3).

4)

in this factory. This is the factory stationary. Some Italian, Russian and other nationalities once were quartered here as slave labor to run this plant. They have some barracks for them in some sort of concentration camp. I am sending my best regards to every one of you, my relatives and friends. I am enclosing a couple of pictures I have taken driving through Germany into Czechoslovakia. Dont look frightened but that is your son. I've got a little something for Jo-ann to take home with me It is not much as there is hardly anything worth having. It is from Czechoslovakia. I have a pair of small shoes for a souvenir which I think I'll send home. They are also from Czechoslovakia. It is 11 o'clock and goodnight. Did you get my packages?

Your loving son,
Gene

P.S. Not in this one, John. Only for sentimental reasons

Letter home (page 4).

Harry Knight,
Mojave Desert.

The taking of
Sgt. Walls
stripes.

Me.

Pyramid tents.

Sunday afternoon.

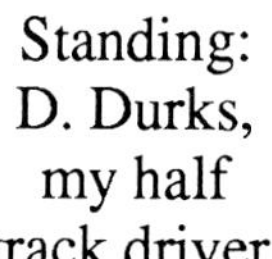

Standing: D. Durks, my half track driver.

Christmas 1942, Mickey Dwyer, me.

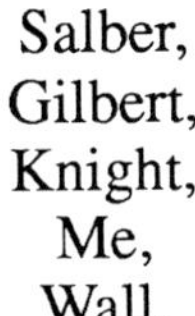

Salber, Gilbert, Knight, Me, Wall.

Knight, Carpenter, Wall, Salber.

speed. Off to my right a tank was burning and then as I glanced to my left, a direct hit knocked out one of our half-tracks with all aboard lost. It was so quick that I lost sight of the half-track as we were high-tailing it out of the situation. Later in the day from our high defense position, a tank battle with our 704th tank destroyer battalion and our tank outfits were maneuvering and firing. Direct hits were scored by each side – smoke and fire,burning tanks and escaping men from the burning vehicles. The losses were great to both sides but the German attack was broken and the battle was over.

This tank battle of Grants, Shermans, and M-18 Tank Destroyers against German Tigers and Panthers is perhaps the greatest tank battle ever waged in the Lorraine Campaign. Many times, in recent years, I discussed the battle with my good friends Patrick Conte and the late John Jesky of the 704th Tank Battalion.

The tankers would often strengthen their vehicles by adding more protection of flat stones and scrap iron to the front of their tanks.

Later that night we took the high ground near Arracourt and in the following day assembled in a small open area. We rested, washed, cleaned up and received a crazy order to police up the area. As we were obeying the order, the Germans were up on high ground miles away and could look down upon us but they were out of range. We were on the defensive, but supplies were not forthcoming. The enemy attacked and shelled us knocking out some vehicles. Some enemy soldiers in foxholes were in our escape path and were no match for our armor as our infantry mopped them up. We were being chased along the Marne Canal by their column and we were shooting at every obstacle to our front. We left piles of enemy ammo along the canal in our haste to be free of the attack and did not have time to destroy any of it. As we were chased, sometime we encountered a small enemy detachment and dispersed them by throwing incendiary grenades into their vehicles. We fought our way into a cemetery and burned some barns with rifle fire into the hay.

On a night counterattack, we moved in total darkness which had some success but it was very frightening as some tankers mistook our armored infantry and fired upon us. We lost some men and only because of our loud cries that we were "Yanks" that they finally stopped. Some enemy soldiers were captured and one G.I. volunteered to take them back to the rear. After they left, and were out of sight, we heard shots and I believe the prisoners were executed. Then, we waited for daylight. The Germans dreaded us and called us "Roosevelt's Butchers" who would shoot, kill, and screw our mothers.

Regrouping, we took up a defensive position and the 10th Armored Infantry Battalion dug in foxholes on the slope of high ground with their vehicles and guns facing the top of the hill. Our company that dug in front of the slope was driven off to the back side of the slope.

Later another company manned the same position we abandoned and were mauled by tanks and infantry. This was when Lt. Field was badly wounded bravely holding off the enemy and an action for which he received "The Medal of Honor".

At this hill, The Germans overran some of our G.I.'s and marched them up to the crest of the hill to try to demoralize us and make us surrender.

Night fell and it was quiet. At early dawn, I left my foxhole to answer nature's call and as I lay my steel helmet on the ground, it was hit by a shot. I went quickly back into the foxhole.

Later in the day, their mortars opened up and some rounds landed in our foxholes. Since I was out in the open checking the line, I jumped into Pedro Villereale's foxhole and landed on top of him when the mortars came in. The foxhole had steel rails across the top with dirt piled high on top. One end of the foxhole had an opening to enter or exit. When an enemy mortar round landed on top and blew the roof off the hole, I felt a piece of hot metal in my foot and also saw the sky. Luck was with me. One mortar round landed in Tec 5 Stephen Mendrey's foxhole, killing him instantly. German tanks with some krauts came over the hill, knocked out all our half-tracks. Thinking this German action was my final goodbye, the end of the road, I half crawled out of Pedro Villerale's foxhole and along with the rest of the squad, tears coming down my face, shooting guns and bazooka's at the attackers, screaming "Come on you sons of bitches, some of you are coming with me!" If they continued to come on, there was nothing to stop them as our artillery fire came later on. In the early morning hours, I spotted an enemy observer on the crest returning to his side of the hill and I shot at him, but I don't know if I hit him.

The 4th Armored Artillery laid down a barrage of fire that held them off. Some of the shells could be seen leaving a trail through the fog, landed very close to (our) foxholes. In the mist shells could be seen in their trajectory before they landed.

During a lull in the fighting and nothing was moving on the battlefield, I immediately checked my platoon and also where our half-track was positioned and where my driver Durkes and his gunner named Rossing were. They were safely dug deep into the earth and were they happy to see it was "Lucky". The soldiers in my company always called me by that nickname. I lost none of my platoon. When I checked our half-track, the (Foolish Virgin), which was demolished, I discovered that all my pictures, camera, $300 worth of francs and spoils of war were destroyed.

Late in the afternoon, I was ordered to take some men and find out the enemy's strength on the other side of the hill. Some of our men were taken prisoner on this hill. Crawling over the crest about 50 yds. or so with the squad, we were fired upon and retreated.

I was called to the Command Post and reported and explained the situation to Capt. Young. I told them that one of our 57mm guns was there, but I didn't know how many of the enemy were there. I did hear some voices. One of the personnel saw that I was bleeding on my hand. It looked like it was a small flesh wound and was taken care of immediately. From this patrol action a call was made for P47's to blast and strafe the position that I described. We held this line till the middle of October, I believe, until we were relieved by the 26th Yankee Division. Andrew Fusco, my friend, was a member of the 26th. Upon leaving this position and my foxhole to a sergeant from the 26th Yankee Division, I took a franc note out of my pocket, signed my name and "Good luck!" and gave the note to him. Leaving the front lines, we assembled and marched back to the rest area with our heads held high and in step past new recruits who were moving up to the line.

Chapter XI

A Rest After 87 Days

For 87 days continuously we were on the front lines and deep inside penetrating enemy areas; we ate only C and K rations until we were finally back in an area where food and showers were provided. In the lull of fighting, our mess Sgt. Kondash slaughtered a pig that the men commandeered and roasted it for the company. Everyone ate heartily but soon after many had stomach cramps and diarrhea. Perhaps these pains were worse than the thought of returning to action. The pain was so severe you almost wanted to die. Thank God the misery passed after a short time. This situation occurred because the meat was not cured, our stomachs had shrunk, and we were not used to eating heavy meals and we were on army rations. For many years, after the greatest conflict in history, I never had an appetite because of this shrinking. The order came down that any leader who thought some men should be sent back home should request it including a reason for the leave. I asked my platoon, but they all wanted to stay. I asked one Pvt. Salvi, how he was doing. He said, "My eyes are not seeing any Germans" and I said to him, "You're going home!" He rebelled, then he accepted. There was another G.I. but I can't remember his name. I learned later Salvi was transferred.

I received a three day pass to Paris, and it was great to get back to life. I stayed with another G.I. named Grammley at the American International Hotel. I never saw so many interesting sights. Paris nightlife was still going strong. I visited Champs-Elysees, Museums, the Eiffel Tower, Follies Begere, Notre Dame Cathedral, Place De Concorde, the banks of the Seine, gardens, and many numerous other places.

Yes, sometimes we had female companionship, but who doesn't during wartime. In all the places where I'd been there were always women for the soldiers and the ladies of Paris were there for Grammley and me, first in my room and then in his. War time can sometimes be fun. There were some close calls on these escapades. In London, I met an Irish lass, perhaps an Irish radical. At night time she brought me up to a waterfront building along the Thames River. Entering the building, there was a man in a bed who looked to be approximately 40 years old. There was no way right there to get any action. I motioned her to jump in with the old man as I felt I was being set-up and ready to be rolled. I left before I took a swim in the Thames. In Germany at the end of the war, I struck up a conversation with an SS wife who was in an early family way. Her husband was a prisoner of war. She entertained me while her father slept in the same room. I woke up later in her bed. It's a wonder he didn't kill me for violating his daughter.

One day when I was in Paris on a pass, an unshaven shavetail (2nd Lieutenant) who I did not know, and I don't believe he knew me, stopped and dressed me down for not saluting him. "What's your name soldier?" I said, "I'm Sgt. Luciano, 4th Arm'd Division." He said, "No you're not." I replied, "Yes, I am!" The lieutenant said, "Why didn't you salute me?" Then without thinking, I blurted out, "You need a shave." He laughed and so did I. I could see now he was feeling no pain.

On the front lines in close contact with the enemy we were careful at times not to salute or show who were the leaders in case of spies or snipers behind our lines. Spit and polish was mostly in rear areas. Although we were clean shaven and washed up by using our helmets, we tried to camouflage anything that was shiny and glittering. Our vehicles, guns, and equipment sparkled in the States and England. In combat, they were clean but not bright so as not to show our positions.

The good times being over, we were back with the outfit outside of Nancy. This was the headquarters of General Patton where he was entertaining the movie star,Marlene Dietrich, in his romantic way. Sgt. Noel greeted me back happily. I spent some time shopping in Nancy and I bought some gifts for my sisters Enes and Ann and especially for my mother. I spent about $40 or more. One was a pin and earrings with the cross of Lorraine and my sisters also received pins.

The USO brought in entertaining shows. One of them was Bing Crosby along with singer, Frances

Langford to entertain the troops. While Bing was singing. some friendly planes flew over, stopping Bing cold. The troops did not move knowing that they were ours, but Bing blurted out, " Are they ours?" Then sensing "all was well", he sheepishly continued singing.

Once in awhile, artillery shells from the long German railroad guns would land in our area.

This was the rainy season and everything was wet and cold although we had shelter in this rest area in the woods outside of Nancy. Other outfits were fighting outside of Metz, but it would be some time before it would be taken.

All this time, I never carried the full weight of equipment on my back. The extra blanket and changes of clothing took their toll on my stature and my weight of 135 pounds. This would have caused me to be fatigued and slow down my movements. The officer asked and practically ordered me to comply with the regulation to help prevent illnesses such as trench feet, which was prevalent. When I explained to the captain the reason for not carrying the equipment, he understood my point of view. The weight carried by a fully equipped soldier is approximately 65 pounds. I carried all the necessary essentials for combat. They were grenades, carbine, bandoliers of ammunition, canteen, shovel, "C" rations and a clean pair of socks. All other articles (blankets, mess kit, gas masks, other changes of clothing and personal items) were left back in the "Foolish Virgin", my half-track.

CHAPTER XII

FENETRANGE, BACK TO ACTION

Now we were ordered to go on the attack again. The artillery and aircraft laid down a heavy barrage before the advance. With the order, "Move out and attack!", the 4th Armored Division began to roll out of their camps and attack. Before this attack, we practiced and had many exercises and dry runs on how to destroy and take the enemy fortified positions. We used plastic explosives, grenades, grenade launchers, and bangalore torpedoes. Bangalore Torpedoes were long pipes with high explosives in them. They were used to blow an opening into enemy fortifications such as wire entanglements, concrete teeth, and pillboxes. Pillboxes were concrete emplacements that were camouflaged and blended into the landscape. They also were made to be concealed among buildings and barns. Their field of fire was extensive for many miles with antitank ditches before them.

As we slowly advanced to complete our mission and take the objective, we moved through and inside the fortified enemy areas.

Then I lost my cool as my B.A.R. gunner was lagging behind. shouted at him, "Get your ass and that gun up to the front and protect those men before I put one through you!"

The terrain was deep mud from the day's rain and streams were flooding the area. Thus our vehicles had difficulty moving across open fields. On roads, anytime I could see fresh broken branches or bits of leaves, I knew danger lay ahead. I suppose it was from shellfire.

Dismounting and attacking beyond some abandoned pillboxes at Fenetrange, we reached the flat of the hill marching on both sides of the road, yards apart between soldiers. Suddenly, enemy fire along with mortar fire from our front fell into our advance, killing two boys near my side and also wounding me. I didn't know I was wounded and kept marching cautiously forward and then I noticed a hole in my combat jacket and a trickle of blood dripping down my arm. Leaving my platoon to others, I marched to the rear to go to a first-aid station as other armed units came up the road. Some of the men on the advancing half-track, many of them I knew, Hollered, "Good Going Lucky!" After the first-aid station, a Red Cross wagon picked me up along with other wounded G.I.'s and brought me to a field hospital. I was feeling faint from the medication or from the wound itself. The hospital was a series of buildings and tents near Chateau Salins. As I entered the building used as a hospital, I saw my cousin Arthur Compito who was from "A" Co. of the 53rd Armored Infantry. I said a few words to him and he said he had foot trouble - trenchfoot. I said, "I'll see you later" as they administered to my wounds. In the morning after breakfast, I tried to locate him - but he was sent out - perhaps home or to England. After some days, I returned to my outfit and took over my platoon. Sgt. Noel who was glad to see me back.

The battles for every foot of ground were costly and men and vehicles were being lost. There were many times when the rains soaked and muddied the ground and many artillery barrages that were shot and some shells became imbedded in the ground without exploding. Even today after fifty years, one hears of a shell exploding when it is disturbed. There were also aerial "bursting" bombs (just at ground level) to inflict heavy casualties on advancing troops. If the enemy shell bursts went into the trees, dangerous splinters were produced. Our company was with General Oden's task force. Our objectives were for Ruhr's industries, towards the Sarre-Union, Sarrbrucken, and Rohrback. In the distance, I could see smoke stacks spewing smoke from their iron and coal factories. On many attacks, civilians would come out of their villages and towns seeking a safer refuge. They were carrying whatever they could manage by carts or on their backs, muttering "Oi,Oi,Oi!" as they fled. Some took refuge in abandoned pill boxes until the attack was over and as we advanced. "War is Hell for everyone!" This is the last area that I was in battle before receiving a furlough home to the states and a well earned rest. At nightfall we would get some rest under the tanks to try to keep warm. Upon awakening, our bodies would be stiff from the cold nights. The medical shots protected us from all types of illnesses. We had wet feet and clothing and resting under tanks, we never went on "sick call". The battle of Rohrback and vicinity was over and we were relieved by the 12th Armored Division. We pulled back into a rest area where a battlefield commission was offered to me but I had to decline it because I was selected to take a stateside furlough that was too good to pass up. S/Sgt. Jackson Vail was also selected for a well deserved furlough from the front lines to bolster the morale, selling of bonds in the States, and touring the war factories at home.

Chapter XIII

Paris, Furlough Home

I took my leave from the outfit about the second week of December. I stayed at the American International Hotel in Paris for about a week or ten days. Arrangements had to be made to fly to England so I had time to take in the sights and the night life of Paris. Ladies of the night were many. They were always propositioning soldiers, especially the Americans who had more money to spend. The night life of Paris carried on as if the war was not going on. Even I forgot about the war as my thoughts were of home.

When the news came that the Boche had made a major attack up through the Ardennes and into the outskirts of Bastogne through our lines and routed some of our green divisions and caused much concern in SHAEF. The line was spread out for many miles and was recently manned by "green" troops of 18 and 19 year old soldiers. One division was our 106th. They were not battle ready to hold off the 5th and the 6th German Panzer Armies. They were mauled and left much of their equipment in hasty retreat. Many lives were lost. All of the U.S. commanders were called to headquarters for what to do. Eisenhower was open to suggestions. General Patton, blustering and boasting said, "I will have the Third Army up to Bastogne in 48 hours!" Here was our General again boasting with "Our Blood and His Guts!"

The Germans were merciless. One German officer on capturing an artillery battalion, marched them out on a field at Malmedy and slaughtered them with machine gun fire. They should have been prisoners of war. We all became apprehensive. Eisenhower thought the Germans were beaten and he even had an early wager with General Montgomery that the war would be over by Christmas of 1944. How wrong the Supreme High Command (SHAEF) was, not to recognize the build-up. General Patton said that the northern armies were not pressing and continuing the attacks giving the Germans time to regroup. SHAEF Headquarters made the greatest mistake by not continuing to press the enemy. The Germans were trying to drive a wedge between the armies towards the Port of Antwerp where most of our supplies were being received. If they were successful, the war would have been of a longer duration unless a negotiated settlement was made. This is what the Germans probably wanted. They failed before on the flight of Rudolf Hess to England for a probable negotiated peace with our leaders. We thought all leaves would be canceled and we would have to return to our units to stem the onslaught of the German breakthrough. The attack was stopped by the holding of the 101st Airborne Division at Bastogne which was an important junction of roads for which the Germans needed to make a further advance to the west and the Port of Antwerp. The 4th Armored Division of the Third Army made one of the greatest feats in war when it broke off from the front in the Saar and raced north over many miles to break the encirclement of Bastogne. The German objectives were doomed and they retreated. This was one of the last attempts by the Germans to regain the initiative. The Battle of the Bulge was a disastrous tactical blunder of our leaders letting the Germans take an advantage by our leaders thinking that they were finished, but it was also one of the greatest military victories by American Forces. The 4th Arm'd Division played a big part.

After enjoying and seeing many interesting places in Paris, orders were for us on leave to fly out on a cargo plane – a Fairchild 47, since most of our aircraft were needed elsewhere. This plane had no navigation equipment and it was to fly us to England. Air activity at this time was dangerous with the German thrust and the Luftwaffe strafing our planes on the ground, perhaps we were fortunate to get this old cargo plane. The airfield was about 20 miles outside of Paris. Our destination in England was to be Birmingham. Why we had to make a forced landing many miles south of our destination, I do not know. The plane dropped altitude immediately as if we were being pursued by attacking forces. We touched down in an open field with a bumpy landing and the English people came out to meet us. We were placed in three-quarter ton vehicles and driven to an airbase. After some discussion, we were marched to a mess hall and had dinner served to us. Since it was getting late into the night, the kitchen staff were really upset to be called to prepare a meal at this late hour.

After dinner, we were loaded on trucks for the long ride to Lichfield. We had Christmas dinner with all the trimmings perhaps on the 28th or 29th of December. We were billeted in Lichfield for about ten days after which we were transported to a port for our journey home to the states.

The ship was the Queen Elizabeth. The trip was uneventful. We were on the water less than a week and landed at the Port of New York and taken to Camp Shanks, New York. The bands were playing, photographers, reporters, and radio people were there to meet us. The newsreel cameras were filming us coming off the ship. These films were shown at a theater later on and it so happened that my sister Enes was at the Warner Theater to see a movie, when the newsreel was projected onto the screen. She shouted and startled the audience by yelling, "That's my brother!"

When we landed we had a terrific meal that was served to us, pictures were being taken, interviews were being given, and telephones were available to call friends and relatives. I think I called home, but I'm not sure. My family already knew that I was coming home through some other source and they held over their Christmas get together. My brother Fred came home from his enlisting in the Air Force and my brother Mario drove in from Hunter's Point Navy Shipyard in San Francisco, California. All of them came to meet me and I was extremely honored and touched. They sent me to Camp Devens, Massachusetts from where I traveled home, I guess by bus. My parents did not know the exact time that I would arrive home and when I knocked on the door and opened it – shouts of glee and happiness from everyone filled the room and with tears running down my mother's face, she hugged me and so did everyone else. I could see the strain on my mother's face. I could see that her hair was much grayer and also she looked a little older. Those telegrams she received when I was wounded overseas must have weighed on her heavily. I could see that my family was proud. My love for my family was never greater. I had more love for everyone now. Before entering the service, I took everything for granted. What is it to say, "I love you", and it is almost like being embarrassed.

Being home, I received many calls from around he country from people asking about their loved ones. I made many calls to my buddies' homes to tell them the messages that were given to me. One visit I made was to Springfield to the home of an officer, who later became my company commander in "A" company. He asked me to visit his wife and his newborn child and give them news about his well-being. He promised me 50 dollars. I also traveled to other G.I.'s towns to give family and friends first-hand news of the front. Because I left the front for about three weeks, I could not tell them what transpired since I left. I took my brother Fred with me as I went along. I also took in some ball games.

I made a few purchases for gifts and gave them out – such as perfume, trinkets and a watch.

I went on a few dates and also palled around with some of my old friends. There were interviews, and writeups on the front pages. I could see from the people that I met on the street, smiles and happiness to see a soldier back from the front lines.

Monsignor William Botticelli from St. Peter's Church came to see me and sat in my mother's kitchen waiting for me to wake up from my first night home. When I told him of my activity in the war, he assured me that we cannot be blamed for the killing and destruction that it causes. Kill or be killed.

The time to report to return to action was drawing near. Happiness in leaving will turn into sadness. "Why do I have to go back?" "Didn't I give my country four years of my life?" Of course the answer was "We need experienced men." I was hoping the war would be over before I returned to my outfit. The war would have been over if Eisenhower refused Montgomery's request for all the supplies. This would have resulted in allowing General Patton's Third Army to continue the assault on the enemy, as Montgomery's Ardennes campaign later failed. Many lives were lost by that mission and later on it gave the Germans time to regroup and attack along the Rhine and then into France and Belgium. "C'est la Guerre", say the French.

Parting from my family was difficult but it had to be done. I had my orders to report to Camp Kilmer, New Brunswick, New Jersey. After arriving we were confined to quarters and barracks, but there was no way they were going to keep me from seeing my family when they came to New York. My parents had relatives in New York and I knew when they were coming down. This order to stay confined to quarters must have come from a "90 day wonder" who had just come out of Officer Training School (O.C.S.) so it seemed. I left the camp – climbed the fence and went into New York and visited with them. If I was apprehended and court martialed – it wouldn't have been too bad, I would have been delayed getting back to the front lines.

I spent the day with my parents and later rode the bus back to camp with no problem. Before we were to move out of our barracks, many soldiers had pent up rages and frustrations so they threw chairs, beds, and bedding out of windows and through the doors of the confining barracks.

Our sailing for England was aboard an old ship called the Aquatania.

As I look back, before returning to the front lines, my sister was keeping company with a nice young man who was in Europe with the Army Engineers. He would later be my brother-in-law, George Kostak.

George's mother asked my sister if we would come and visit her and we did at the end of January. My sister introduced me to the family who later on, would also be my in-laws.

They asked me about certain happenings and what it was like although I couldn't tell them anything about their son. The ones that were there included my future brother and sister-in-law, mother and father-in-law, and my future wife and her three year old daughter. She had recently lost a fine man, her husband of not many years.

With me were my sisters, Frances Toro, and a cousin from New York.

For some unknown reason, my future wife did not take kindly to me and walked away into the kitchen with her daughter. This did not matter to me as the rest of the family was friendly, otherwise I would have left. I felt rudeness on her part, but I have forgiven her as her mind was elsewhere. In peacetime it was a different air about the past which I will narrate later.

Sailing out of New York, I was very apprehensive. When I left Boston on the Thomas Barry in December, 1943, all of us were very excited and proud to be shipping overseas and not realizing that some would never return. Now that I'm returning, the feeling of going into combat, after seeing so much destruction and death, did not excite me. Remembering back in Chippenham recalling what the officer said, "You might be buying the farm." It could be a reality.

Chapter XIV

Back To France, Joining "A" Company

Landing in Scotland off the Aquatania, I headed for the train for the southern port of embarkation to sail on an L.C.I. (Landing Craft Infantry), and I bumped into Virgil Parducci from Torrington. "What are you doing here?" The reply was the same from each of us since we were both here for the same reason. It was a surprise that someone from home was on the same rail platform as I was, far away from home. On boarding the L.C.I. boats, the English were in charge and we were below decks. If we were torpedoed – forget it and goodbye – "Till we meet again."

Trying to eat on upright stationary tables was a chore. The messkit had to be held firmly as the ship bobbed and swayed back and forth. Our menu consisted of lamb's tongue and many of the boys were seasick. The English went through difficult times, suffered immensely, and still endured with an iron will through all the bombing.

The L.C.I. docked onto the beach in Le Havre, France and we marched up the beach into the outskirts of the city. Lo and Behold! Going to the church, a wedding party passed us. Strange, even war could not delay their love. From here, into a camp we marched. The camp was well camouflaged in the woods.

After a few days, arrangements were made to ride a transport vehicle back to a "repo depo" from where we would rejoin our outfit. The replacement area were barracks in the city of Metz. They perhaps housed Germans before we captured them.

A roll call was made everyday for certain persons to rejoin their outfit. My name was never called and I wasn't in any hurry to get back to the front because I didn't know how I would react to events that I had previously participated in.

But the wait was getting to me and I asked them to send me up to my outfit. To my surprise they didn't know or have my records but they did oblige me by sending me to the 4th Armored Division, 10th Armored Infantry, "C" Company. I caught up with the outfit on the other side of the Rhine River, crossing on a pontoon bridge.

On the day that I joined "C" Company, we were strafed by enemy aircraft and also shelled by enemy artillery. It took a little while for me to readjust. I was frightened, as if I was entering combat for the first time, but my fright would never be shown to my buddies. At this time, changes had to be made in the makeup of the companies. "A" Company was on a mission into enemy lines and never got back to the outfit until much later. They were on Capt. Baum's foray to rescue war prisoners including Patton's son-in-law, Colonel Waters. This was the prisoner of war camp, Stalag (XIII C) at Hammelburg. The mission was a disastrous undertaking with not enough vehicles to bring back the rescued prisoners; so a new "A" Company had to be formed. I was selected with Sgt. Wineburger and Captain Tessier to form the new "A" Company with some of the original "A" Company's soldiers and some replacements – raw recruits. Armand Pollutro, who had been sent to England because of trench feet, rejoined the outfit and he was assigned as my half-track driver. We were together in the beginning at Camp Croft, and now in the end, we were rejoined on the battlefield in Germany.

The Lieutenant was new in my platoon and he let me take charge of the platoon's movements.

Their O.C.S. training taught them basic military lessons but on the battlefield, one had to react according to the situation. Therefore it was I who was responsible for the deployment and advance of my men during our attacks.

With the 10th Armored Infantry Battalion leading, we attacked the towns of Weimar, Jena, Gotha and Ohrdruf.

Many German soldiers lay dead in ditches along the sides of the roads as we advanced. Our Air Force, artillery and bombs were destroying and demoralizing their will to fight. There was very little resistance. Their reserves were depleted. Many old men and very young boys were called up to fill their ranks.

In Gotha, we were getting sporadic fire from a factory, we blasted the building with bazooka, small arms fire, and we cleared out the snipers and captured the town.

The blaring sound trucks delivering ultimatums to the German people in their cities and towns were used to pressure them for their immediate surrender. They were being warned to comply or they would be attacked and bombed. Many times, in the last stages of the war, white sheets would be hanging from the windows surrendering before we arrived. Many houses in some of the towns were commandeered for billets for our troops.

Chapter XV

Concentration Camp, Gotha, Jena

At Gotha, since "A" Co had new soldiers, they were given training in firing bazooka's, mortars, guns and the reading of the "Articles of War".

One of the first concentration camps was at Ohrdruf. The guards and the officials of the concentration camp, desperate not to be caught, fled at our approaching attack and did not have time to kill the rest of the emancipated prisoners. These prisoners, at our approach, rushed out of the gates waving their arms ecstatically at us as our vehicles entered the open gates of the camp. Many prisoners, laid in their bunks too weak to move, but raised their arms in thanks. Bodies were piled high on the ground, others were in pits covered with lime. There were rows of ditches filled with buried bodies with an occasional leg or arm protruding out of the ground. The stench was intolerable. I don't believe there were ovens for burning corpses here, but I saw them somewhere. It was a very gruesome sight. Many of our higher officers viewed this scene. General Patton was so disgusted that he ordered the Burgermeister, his wife, and all the inhabitants of the town witness this atrocity. Many said they never knew, though a pungent odor drifted into town. Seeing this inhuman slaughter, the Burgermeister, his wife and many other town people took their own lives. After reviewing this destruction of humanity, "Was there any reason for not fighting the evil Nazi regime?"

After a few days of instructions and drills, we were on the march occasionally receiving sniper fire.

Marching – of course that is riding in half-tracks – we came to an outskirt of Gotha. All was quiet and nothing was in our way except off in the distance, on a sloping hill towards us, was an elderly civilian waving something. As he was coming towards us and before I could react, my half-track gunner on the 50 caliber gun fired and he fell. I showed my displeasure, but I did not make a case out of it. This was war and my gunner was new. It could have been that the man was going to surrender the area so we wouldn't damage their property. The platoon halted in front of the town after dismounting and did not move. The platoon moved in a spread out formation, not in a skirmish line but on each side of the road. I went forward and they followed. After I smashed some locked doors with the butt of my carbine, they got the message and followed suit. Resistance was minor so we passed along the road before our half-tracks came up for us to mount-up. As our half-tracks came to us, out of the sky we were strafed by our own planes. We quickly put out our marking cloth panels to let them know we were friendly. The panel colors were changed from day to day so that friendly forces would know friend from foe. It would not help the enemy because they would never know the color for that day. We lost one man to the strafing. As the strafing went on, we rushed into the cellars of homes, but in a few minutes it was all over.

Later we crossed the Saale River at Jena on April 20, 1945 and bivouacked for the night after putting out outposts. This was my 29th birthday.

The next day, we rode on top of tanks to attack the town ahead of us where enemy activity could be seen. As we were advancing, the tank that I was riding, stopped as we approached barbed-wire entanglements. I do not know if he thought it was booby-trapped. Forgetting my own safety, I jumped off the back of the tank and cut the wire with my wire-cutters and pushed it aside. Remounting the tank, we rode to the outskirts of the town, dismounted, and continued our attack.

The enemy opened up with artillery, mortars, and grenade launchers. They also were dug into foxholes.

As we attacked on foot, racing through their positions and routing them, we captured the town. The shots were coming from foxholes. They were throwing panzerfausts which were large grenade-like bombs that looked like potato mashers. We killed and captured them out of foxholes. Some were young boys. The Germans were at the bottom of their reserve and conscripting young boys and old men. They were finished, but they could still inflict misery, pain, injury and killing Americans. As I led my platoon, I would take the butt of my gun and smash plate glass windows of stores and enter and investigate them. I could hear shots whistle past me and splatter up against buildings. I moved up the left side of the road on the attack and another sergeant led the right side. We lost one man to rifle fire. Our mission was to clear all buildings of any enemy resistance. My platoon on the left side of the street moved while watching the buildings on the right side of the street, entering and clearing them. Troops on the other side of the street did the same thing. One home I entered later on was searched, but we found nothing. At first the people cowered, but were relieved to see we weren't going to harm them. Most of the town people cowered into cellars. As we were entering a cellar, voices were heard and we found many civilians huddled together. I told them I wasn't there to hurt them, "Just tell me if there are any soldiers here?" They responded with "Nein". I checked them and they were relieved so we moved on mopping up the town and commandeering houses for billets for our troops. The German civilians in this house were scared. After setting up a defensive line, I took shelter in a house that we commandeered. At nightfall, I found a feather duster and letting the German civilians lay in their beds, I went to sleep. In the middle of the night, I was awakened by one of my sergeants escorting a German soldier who had surrendered. I awoke the civilians and turned him over to their custody and held them responsible if he escaped. In the morning I sent the German back to headquarters to be interrogated. As I was sitting in their living room, the lady of the house ushered in her daughter and practically offered her to me. She cupped one hand around her daughter's breast and sort of smiled to me and nodded. I looked at her and motioned to her that she was pretty and shook my head. I believe that she and her daughter were relieved. I asked the mother if she had some eggs and to cook them for us which she did.

On one of our attacks, there was sniper fire and believing it was coming from a beautiful mansion, I was ordered to check it out. Armand Pollutro stopped his half-track and we dismounted. We entered through a garden gate and circling the house, I entered the house with a couple of soldiers. Inside was a well dressed lady and over her objections, I told her what we were looking for. We searched the whole building and came up empty. We left and rejoined our outfit.

There were times when we had to throw grenades into hiding places, but I am thankful this was not one of them. I know that happened in St. Genevieve (I think that was the name of the town), when one of our soldiers killed a woman and her 2 children by throwing a grenade into their dugout shelter.

Some locked stores and homes were smashed open with the butts of our guns – smashed doors and plate glass windows.

After clearing the town of resistance, we moved to the outskirts and dug in. Looking off in the distance, the enemy was also digging in to our front and when they realized we were close at hand, they retreated. Now, evening was falling and security had to be set up for our unit so I placed my platoon below the crest of a hill with two men in each outpost, 50 yds. apart.

The enemy vehicles could be heard retreating over the crest of the hill. I setup my command post at the bottom of the hill. In the early morning hours the next day, I pulled in our outpost to be on our way. The column never seemed to get started so we waited. Another sergeant and I lay down on a grassy hillside and fell asleep for a short snooze. Imagine our surprise when we awoke and found that we were alone among German civilians.

A vehicle came by and we joined our outfit and entered a bivouac area.

Now we were not going to advance to the east as we later heard the deal was for the Russians to meet us at the Elbe River. Looking off in the distance, I could see a town with smoke coming out of a stack. I believe it was Chemnitz. If Patton's 3rd Army was not stopped at the Elbe, he probably with his boasting, get to Berlin and fulfill his promise of kicking Hitler in the ass. This "Our Blood and Guts!"

It was now that we heard about our President's death and we wondered about the war with Japan.

The enemy was now recruiting young boys and old men, perhaps women also – though I never saw any of them except for other duties like our women did in service.

We had a feeling that the war was near its end, but dangers to oneself were still possible. Now was the

Coming home, October 1945, with 9th arm'd.

My 27th birthday at the Biltmore Bowl, Los Aneles, California.

Return to Pine Camp 1992.
Left to right: Noel, me, Mills, Chalfont,
Stickford, Grbovac.

2nd Platoon Barracks.

Watertown, New York, south of Pine Camp.

Sister Enes, Daughter Katherine.

A TORRINGTON VETERAN along with other Yanks catch up on the news following their arrival at the New York port of embarkation from overseas. They are among 1300 veterans of the First, Third and Ninth Armies fighting in the European theater, who were given furloughs as a reward for numerous decorations and outstanding battle performance. Left to right: SGT. EUGENE LUCIANO, Torrington, SGT. JACK LAMB, Lawrence, Mass., who was wounded twice; SGT. ARTHUR E. MARTELL, Hempstead, N. H., and PFC. FRANK J. CALITRI, Hartford, who was wounded twice.—AP Photo.

Cousins Wounded In Action

Pfc. Arthur Compito, left, and Staff Sgt. Eugene Luciano, cousins, were wounded in action recently in France. They entered the army together July 1, 1941, and were serving with an armored division. Sgt. Luciano has recovered and returned to duty Dec 1, according to word received by his parents, Mr. and Mrs. Antonio Luciano, 277 East Main street. Pfc. Compito formerly made his home with the Lucianos.

Brings Word From Hometown Buddies On Western Front

By Special Correspondent

Torrington, Jan. 16—T/Sgt. Eugene Luciano, 28, one of the 1,368 wounded and decorated heroes to return from the Western front on 30-day merit furloughs, arrived home today bearing messages from five Torrington buddies whom he left behind.

The soldier, twice wounded within a month, served overseas 13 months in England and France with an armored division of the Fourth Army.

The armored infantryman, son of Mr. and Mrs. Anthony Luciano, 237 East Main St., saw some "rough and tough fighting," he related, in half-tracks through the Normandy hedgerows. His unit moved from 50 to 60 miles a day until reaching the Metz area where the pace was slowed down by enemy barbed wire and enemy aircraft fire, he said.

Other Torrington men in his battalion, whose families Sgt. Luciano plans to visit while home, are Arthur Pergo'a, Armand Pollutro, Philip Cianciolo, Patrick Quinn and Paul Persechino. They are "all okay" he reported, and none of the Torrington boys in his outfit was injured in combat.

While riding in a tank, the sergeant's commanding officer approached to tell him he was going to the "zone of the interior." Sgt. Luciano, hearing the news about his furlough home, thought his captain was kidding at first.

Sgt. Luciano spent New Year's eve in Paris awaiting plane transportation to England, and visited his cousin, Arthur Compito, ill in a hospital in France, before coming home.

The sergeant was wounded Oct. 6 and Nov. 25, and returned to duty Dec. 1. He wears the Purple Heart with an Oak Leaf Cluster.

A graduate of Torrington high school, class of '34, Sgt. Luciano was employed by the Hendey Machine Co. before entering the Army four years ago. He went overseas in December, 1943. He will report Feb. 15 at Fort Devens, Mass.

1,368 Soldiers Arrive Home From Battlefields

Decorated Heroes Happy Over 30-Day Merit Furloughs

By HELEN CAMP

New York, Jan. 13—(AP)—Today 1,368 men are home from the battlefields in Europe.

They came from Germany, Belgium, France, Italy, Sicily—and they are on their way to Pennsylvania, Texas, Utah and points north, south, east and west.

The interval in between—the first day those 1,368 men had spent on American soil in anywhere from six months to three years—was a crazy kaleidoscope of sights and sounds and emotions.

It was the boy who reached out to brush my cheek lightly with his hand as he stepped off the gangplank in New York harbor and said softly and impersonally, "An American girl! It's wonderful!"

It was the ruddy-faced lieutenant colonel on the train to Camp Shanks who fumbled for official words to describe how it felt to be back in America and then broke into a little-boy grin and exclaimed: "I wish I could sing."

It was the way a soldier looked at a huge T-bone steak in the Camp Shanks mess hall.

And it was the bitter, steely-eyed look on the scarred face of one infantryman who said almost hysterically, "I don't want my biography in no papers. I just don't, that's all."

The 1,368 men comprised the largest group of non-casualties yet to be sent back from the combat zones. They were from the 12th Army group and had served with the 1st, 3d and 9th armies.

All had been decorated, some as many as 10 or 12 times. They were hand-picked for 30-day merit furloughs according to their length of service and number of decorations, evacuations, and wounds.

Some will be discharged, for dependency reasons, for medical reasons, for Army reasons. Others will be shipped back to combat duty. The majority will be labeled for "T.D."—Temporary duty within the United States.

They arrived in New York as only returned GIs could arrive in New York.

They jammed the decks of their troop transport in a raw waterfront wind, some bareheaded, one shirt-sleeved, all dancing and shouting and smiling.

They waved captured swastika flags. They tossed European coins onto the docks. They whistled at pretty girls, plain girls, any girls. They booed MPs. They shouted at the band for jive music. And they drank milk and milk and more milk and marveled at the miracle of milk.

"Hey, Blondie!"

"Hey, do me a favor, will ya?

Family Can't Believe Gene's Coming Home

Torrington Soldier, Shot Twice, Among Returning Veterans

By Special Correspondent

Torrington, Jan. 13 — A twice-wounded Torrington veteran of 13 months' overseas service was among the 1,368 heroes who arrived in New York on 30-day mer t furloughs.

T/Sgt. Eugene Luciano, 28, wrote his last letter home Nov. 28 from a hospital in France. The next word from him was a telegram with the surprise message, "Have arrived in the States."

The soldier's sister, Miss Enes Luciano, had to have the message

Picture on Page 3.

repeated twice. "Gene's" parents. Mr. and Mrs. Anthony Luciano, 237 East Main St., laughing and crying at the same time, were "lost for words."

"We still can't believe it," his sister said tonight.

The sergeant, expected home in a day or two, served with an armored infantry division of Patton's Third Army in France. He was wounded Oct. 6 and Nov. 25, and had returned to duty Dec. 1. He wears the Purple Heart with an Oak Leaf Cluster.

A graduate of Torrington high school, class of '34, Sgt. Luciano was employed by the Hendey Machine Co. before entering the Army four years ago. He went overseas in December, 1943 and served in England before arriving in France last July. He was prominent here as a baseball player, both at school and on independent teams.

A brother, Aviation Cadet Orlando Luciano, 18, entered service Friday and is now at Fort Devens, Mass.

Other Connecticut soldiers in the group are Pvt. Clifford Eberhardt of Stamford, Pfc. Frank J. Calitri of Hartford, and Cpl. Joseph Sansevero of Northford.

Three Reported Wounded During Europe Action

Three Torrington soldiers have been wounded in action in the European theater of operations, according to information received by their families.

Pvt. Myles H. Jenney was seriously wounded in Germany in December, according to a war department telegram received by his wife, the former Marion B. Tieman of Bakerville.

Pvt. Jenney, son of Mr. and Mrs. Frank Jenney of Daytona Beach, Fla., entered the service last March and has been serving overseas several months. He served with the infantry.

Staff Sgt. Eugene Luciano, son of Mr. and Mrs. Antonio Luciano, 237 East Main street, was wounded Nov. 25 in France, according to a war department telegram received by his family yesterday.

His cousin, Pfc Arthur Compito, who entered the army with him July 9, 1941, and served in the same armored division of the Third Army, also was wounded, and has written home that he met Eugene in a hospital Nov. 26. Pfc. Compito formerly lived with the Lucianos.

Sgt. Luciano, who has been overseas since December, 1943, also was slightly wounded in action on Oct. 1.

Spearheaded Drive Of Patton's Army Against Germans

Several Torrington soldiers are serving with an armored division of Gen. Patton's Third Army, which spearheaded that army's advance across France to the vicinity of Saarburcken in a steady drive on Nazi war factories of the Saar basin.

Torrington men listed on the division's roster include Sgts. Patrick Quinn, Eugene Luciano and Henry Kaczmarczyk; Corps. Armand Pollutro, Philip Cianciolo and Paul Perscchino and Pfc. Arthur Pergola.

The division was activated at Pine Camp, N. Y., April 15, 1941, landed in France the week of last July 12, and began fighting five days later. During its drive across France, it smashed 400 enemy tanks, knocked out 1,500 miscellaneous vehicles and took 15,000 captives, at relatively low cost to itself, the war department has announced.

Once turned loose in France, the unit forced crossings of the Selune, Leing, Yonne, Seine, Marne, Meuse, Moselle and Meurthe rivers, any one of which would have been a tough tactical problem alone.

After crossing the Moselle, north and south of Nancy, the division

(Continued On Page Thirteen)

Spearheaded Drive

(Continued From Page Five)

met and repulsed the heaviest tank attacks in the battle of France. In Brittany, the unit is known as the "Liberators of Brittany".

Jumping off in Normandy July 27 after intense air and infantry attacks on the enemy front, the division cut off the Brittany peninsula in ten days; raced through Porters; took Coutances and Sartilly; captured the key city of Avranches after savage fighting, plunged into Brittany to march alone 140 miles to contain Rennes and capture Vannes on the south coast of Brittany; took Nantes and contained Lorient, the Nazi submarine base, in a move that trapped thousands of Nazis.

From Brittany, the unit turned east and dashed 163 miles in two nights and a day, capturing Orleans and outflanking Paris from the south. It resumed its drive and dashed to Sens, where the garrison was caught unprepared and enormous quantities of supplies were captured. Then one group crossed the Yvonne river to destroy an SS brigade on the outskirts of Villeneuve, while another group, traveling south, captured Courtenay and moved on Montargis from the east.

The division fought its way across the Seine and attacked Troyes, fighting under heavy enemy fire but destroying 60 per cent of an enemy brigade. Three days later the division had made three crossings of the Marne and captured Vitry-le-Francois. Chalon-sur-Marne, St. Dizler and Ligney fell rapidly. A light tank company took Commercy, captured the bridge across the Meuse and seized high ground to the east.

Meanwhile, a combat group of the division, supported by an infantry division, burst across the Moselle, routing azis ordered to hold the line all winter. While the massive Moselle bridgehead was being consolidated, the unit fought off some of the heaviest German attacks of the war and, during two weeks, threw back Nazi tank units with heavy losses to the enemy.

In addition to two Distinguished Service Crosses, Silver Stars have been awarded to 114 members of the division for gallantry in action and 406 men have been presented with Bronze Stars for heroic action and meritorious service.

time to be careful.

The scuttlebutt was the German's attempt to make a last stand in the Austrian Redoubt, but it never came to pass.

Orders were to head for Czechoslovakia into Prague. We entered the country and bivouacked for the night. The next day, orders were not to advance to Prague because the Russians were going to take the city.

This was a happy situation for the troops, as we knew the war would soon be over. Why risk our lives?

Can you imagine what a different world it would have been if we had taken Berlin and Prague instead of the Russians?

We marched in columns through the Czecho-slovakian town of Sussice and other towns with the populace waving small flags as their Liberators passed. They were jubilant to be free of the mistreatment and hardships of the enemy occupation.

We moved into Pole, Czechoslovakia and here we remained. The war in Europe was over! Now came the occupation.

At Pole, our duty was to restore order, patrol the occupation area and take care of any problems that arose with the populace. I was honored with a ceremony for Company "A" and received the Commendation and Merit Award. From our area, passes were given to Sussice and other points of interest. We drilled, had classes and received medals such as the Combat Infantry Badge. There were also troop reviews such as the one called by General

Patton. Medals were given out for acts of bravery, for good leadership, and for completing and being efficient in the performance of duties. Many of the soldiers who made the supreme sacrifice never received any medals. They are the ones we are indebted to. Many enlisted men and officers received medals that they really weren't entitled to, but were written up in glowing terms (by their superiors) that were sent onto their headquarters.

The medal that stands out beside the Congressional Medal of Honor is the Purple Heart and the Combat Infantry Badge. Officers back of the lines, had medals hanging on their jackets from the top of the shoulder to their belt line. I suppose they received them for the deeds their men did up on the front lines and for the ones that are in hallowed ground. I totally agree.

The farm houses had thick walls of concrete, plaster and stone and some had manure piles in front of them to fertilize their fields. When it rained the stench from the manure was awful as the water would run down the deep ditches along the dirt roads. The occupants of these houses had horse drawn wagons with barrels or buckets which they used to irrigate their fields.

Some of the small towns in this locale had crucifixes on hillsides as places to pray.

We left this area to begin our tour of duty as the Army of Occupation in the American Zone. On the banks of the Danube, the town of Kelheim, Germany was to be our occupation zone. This was once a place where a stalag for Italian and other war prisoners was located. There were salt mines in this area along with the large Krupp Steel Works where forced labor was used. The barracks used by the slave laborers were very poorly constructed but were now ours. It was our duty to clean, repair and wash everything in these shacks. This included removing the prisoner's graffiti from the walls, installing wood over dirt floors, and putting in bunk beds. We also had to cleanup the courtyard, make a rock garden around the walkways, and construct and raise a flagpole.

The final result had a peaceful atmosphere compared to what had gone on before. We were now part of the Occupation Army of Germany. We had a certain area to patrol, checking displaced person to see whether any Nazi officials were trying to flee among the displaced persons. My assignment was a radius of fifty miles which I traveled with some men and vehicles. Some of the time, we pitched a pyramidal tent and stayed in one place before moving on to a new locale.

On one of these missions, we pitched a tent some miles from Kelheim and we took turns patrolling the area for a week. On one of these patrols a young deer crossed a short distance from us and I fired but the gun jammed. I took unmerciful ribbing from some recruits. After I corrected my gun problem, I stated to them, "See that slender birch tree out there?" The tree was about 200 yds. away. "Just watch." I pulled the trigger and shot and said, "Go take a look." Hell, I wasn't sure I hit it. They signalled a hit. I was relieved.

That was the last time I ever challenged anyone about my shooting.

At camp or the company area, there were classes, drills, nomenclature of weapons, reveilles and retreats. As this phase of my patrolling ended, I was placed in charge of a prisoner of war camp outside of Kelheim.

Upon taking up the duty of the enclosure, I rimmed the sunken camp with machine gun outposts and there was a wire fence at the far end. This was a large excavation – perhaps as large as a football field. It probably was at one time being mined and dug out for, as some said, a salt mine. The laborers had been Italian prisoners of war.

After a few days of my duty, I called on the leader (interpreter) of the prisoners that I would have an inspection of all gear and equipment that the prisoners had in their possession. I told him to have all of his men in front of their tents and put everything out in the open. At the beginning of the inspection before entering into the sunken pit, a couple of prisoners raised an objection and I was so enraged that my men had to calm me down or I might have blown them away with my carbine. The interpreter warned his men to stop the rebelling or suffer the consequences of the incident. The inspection went off as planned and much contraband was confiscated. Among the items were many pistols, rifles, a German machine gun, cameras and typewriters. Every day people outside of the compound asked about the prisoners, especially women who somehow knew that some relative of theirs was in the prisoner of war enclosure. I did not have the authority at this time to let them see any prisoners. I told them to leave and not make matters more difficult for themselves. Since these prisoners were regular army and not S.S. soldiers, they would soon be processed and then released. This duty lasted three weeks before I returned to Kelheim quarters. The rumor mill had some of us going to fight the Japanese.

I also was called to attend a class of officers on a review of army procedures to demonstrate the changing and posting of the guards. The procedures of posting and changing of the guard, the Sgt. of the guard would march the new guard detail in formation to relieve guards that were on duty. The posts were 2 hours on and 4 hours off. Changing from one detail to the new guard detail, standing at attention in formation, the officer of the day would order "Post". The sergeant of the guard would move to the front of the detail, salute the officer and march off with the new guard. The old guard is then dismissed. He would post a guard and have the old guard fall in behind him. When all posts were changed, they would return to the guard house. If a problem on the post occurred, the sentry would shout, "Sgt. of the guard!", who would immediately investigate.

The point system was established for returning soldiers to the States. It was for time served and awards. And having 101 points, which meant I would not have to wait very long, I considered and decided against accepting the rank of 1st Sgt. Knowing that I was soon to leave and having 101 points might have disrupted my return to civilian life. Also my duties were less and less, so I recommended one of my squad leaders, Ray Fratacangelo for the post. Later, the company also fell out to honor me for the Army Commendation Medal.

Chapter XVI

Fraternization And Occupation

I was transferred to the 9th Armored Division to be redeployed. The 4th Armored Division was to remain as part of the Army of Occupation. The feeling of leaving was emotional. I had been with my buddies a long time. I made my farewell parting words with them all and entered a new phase of my army life.

We traveled many miles and moved into the town of Markleuthen and billeted in a schoolhouse across from the Rathaus.

My unit was Company "A", 27th Armored Infantry, 9th Armored Division. Our company commander took over a house from some Germans and asserted himself by firing two shots into the floor when they tried to talk him into not taking over their house. They then understood him.

During the day, I would take walks into the fields and around the small village. People were bicycling and working in the fields. Food was rationed and times were very difficult for them. We did what we could to help them. One day, walking in a field with my carbine slung over my shoulder, I came across a young lady stretched out on a blanket sunning herself and reading a book. She was very beautiful and athletic looking. After I showed that I was friendly and not there to harm her, she finally said hello. She explained that she had served in the service of Germany. Being uncomfortable, she left me and I went upon my way. Days later, she and her friend were walking down the street in front of the schoolhouse and she was much more at ease. She invited me up the street to her house a little away from the schoolhouse. The house was well kept and her mother had religious pictures around the house. Her name was Martha Braun. She sat on the window sill and strummed her guitar and sang. She looked very angelic there. Her picture in her uniform, was on the table. I liked her immensely.

Years later when I recalled some of those times, I was thinking, far fetched of course, but that I was born on April 20 and so was Hitler, 26 years before me. He had a friend who he married later on named Braun and my friend was Braun. A small coincidence, but amusing.

At one time we were billeted in a large chalet in a beautiful park. I do not remember if it was before Markleuthen or before coming to my new location in the city of Hof.

From Markheuthen I was billeted in a large hotel in Hof and down the street was a brewery. This seemed to be a place of some activity.

This was like a vacation with nothing to do but take in the sights and play. Fraternizing with the ladies was "verboten" but we did it anyway. My friend from Markleuthen used to come up to see me. I tried to not see her, but to no avail. I knew that nothing could come of the situation.

One night all the soldiers had friends in their hotel rooms when our company commander came busting into the hotel. From his voice, I believe he was drunk and lonely. He started on the first floor smashing in locked doors and shouting at and rounding up girls and taking names of the soldiers. He then did the same on the second floor.

There was no way I could get my friend out. I decided to unlock the door and put her into a stand-up clothes closet and locked it. I opened the bathroom door, neatly folded my clothes and pulled the covers up to my chin facing the wall. The door slammed up against the wall as he entered my room. He must have been surprised the door wasn't locked. He must have been confused because he looked around the room and bathroom and then tried the closet door,stopped and left my room. I still wonder why he didn't break the closet door lock or shout at it. Did he let me win? I worry now years later, that if I had been caught with someone in my room, I would have been busted down to the rank of Private.

All the girls and soldiers were punished. The girls were turned over to civil authorities and many of the soldiers lost their rank.

The food problem was critical for the German people. Many young people would station themselves ouitside of the army mess halls and at the garbage cans scrounging for food from soldiers mess-kits before disposal. Some of us would leave some food in our mess-kits and give it to the unfortunates. There were those whose hate was so strong because of losing a buddy that they would grind a cigarette butt and spit into the food before emptying their mess-kit.

I socialized with many German people. I met an elderly couple near the government buildings and they invited me to their home and had a friendly conversation. At one point, they asked if I could get some meat for them. I knew someone who handled rations and I was able to get them a small piece of meat. They offered me some old coins, but I wouldn't take them, so they gave me a pair of binoculars.

Somehow, I obtained a nice set of Bavarian china dishes. I had a crate made by a German carpenter to have the dishes shipped home. After having them packed and addressed, we then received orders to leave the hotel in Hof and prepared to move out for the Lucky Strike camp in Marseilles, France. I asked a soldier to ship them home for me. He shipped them out alright, but not to my home. One officer even sent a piano and many other things to his home. Many of my new friends, including ones from Markleuthen came to see us leave; even an S.S. wife who entertained me one lonely night.

We were transported by trucks to a staging area. I can't remember if we went by train or on Army vehicles to Camp Lucky Strike in Marseilles, France.

At Hof, we had many good times. At Regensburg and Bayeruth, we saw many U.S. shows and at

Berchtesgaden, we saw Hitler's Eagle Nest. The best show was Billy Rose's Diamond Horseshoe Show.

Now we were in southern France, waiting for ships to take us to our next adventure. Is it Japan for us? Of course no one of the soldiers was enthused by that prospect.

At this camp on French soil, we were housed in Pyramidal tents, but the waiting for weeks was very discouraging. Movies were shown every night down a mountainside gently sloping to the screen.

Finally, the day came for us to move to the docks. We knew now that Japan was out of the question because they had surrendered. THE LARGE BOMB was the "Last Hurrah" for Japan and also the Russians entered the last week of the war. We never knew until later that Japan surrendered because of the Atomic Bomb.

Chapter XVII

End Of Army Life

I sailed on the S.S. America with many 9th Armored Division soldiers and other units in September. Rotation for going home was on the point system such as length of service, time overseas, medals, and injuries. Since I had 101 pts, I was one of the fortunate ones to leave in September. The moods were many aboard ship, happiness, sadness, thoughtfulness and pride. All kinds of activities were taking place. Money was being won and lost. Some were getting richer, some were broke and poor, but still they were happy to be heading home. The food on the ship was fine. We sailed into Newport News, Virginia at night and debarked. People were lining the gangplanks, bands were playing, flags were waving, and suddenly walking down onto the docks, soldiers would straighten up, throw back their shoulders and march proudly by all of the well wishers. I felt chills and a heartfelt feeling raced through my frame. I am proud of my accomplishments and I am home. We entrained to Fort Devens where we received lectures and offers of incentives to join the Reserve (two thousand dollar bonus).

These have been the main events of my army life. As I wrote these memoirs, I began recalling more and more of these events and incidents that occurred to me.

In my haste for my separation, I made the mistake of not staying until I put in an application for benefits for my back troubles from combat and the continual ringing in my ears from my time at the firing range. Also, I needed dental work which I had done shortly after returning home. Now, going home, I recalled some remarks from General Patton who used our blood and his guts saying to tell our grandchildren, "Son, your grand- daddy rode with the great Third Army and that son of a bitch named Patton!"

Oh so what the hell! It's done! 54 months of service. Let me go home! I have had enough! I am a veteran.

After my discharge from the army, I applied for the 52-20 that soldiers were to receive to readjust to civilian life. After receiving one payment of $20, payment was stopped. The reason was because I would not accept a job at 25 cents an hour at a laundry for which I was qualified for in civilian life. At my hearing, I was so upset because I was rejected and blurted out, "Lady, while I'm out there dodging bullets and you're here sitting on your ass, telling me that I have to take what is offered to me, Shove It!"

Naturally, I never received any help and so with the help of my savings, I started my own business. The returning soldiers of WWII never received the parades and accolades that the soldiers of recent wars received. "C'est la guerre, C'est la vie!"

Chapter XVIII

Training and Induction

On July 9, 1941 we were called to answer for induction into the armed forces to be present at the Torrington City Hall. With most of our families being present, we were greeted by Mayor William A. Patten who gave us a welcoming and a send-off speech. My cousin Arthur Compito was going to be inducted later but then decided to be inducted with my group. We were loaded onto a bus for the trip to Hartford and arrived there about noon. The "swearing in" to the Army took place there and the Articles of War were read to us. These Articles of War were read to us many times during the war.

Aboard a train, we were transported to Fort Devens near Ayer, Massachusetts. Upon entering the fort, we were issued Army uniforms and fatigues. There were many classes and lectures given by medical personnel, as well as shots and checkups by many Army doctors. This is also when I first learned about "peter inspections". We were all assembled in a single line wearing only a raincoat and shoes for the examination by the doctor who sat on a stool and gave the most embarrassing review of our private parts.

How we "toed the line" on commands and

orders! We were harassed and made to comply to the silliest of orders. When the bugler played, "Lights out" and Taps at nine o'clock, we thought we had to be in bed at that time. Later on we understood that we could be anywhere on the grounds. After a fortnight, we left aboard a train for Camp Croft, South Carolina. It was exciting to travel on such a long train ride and seeing the country along the way. At the railroad station we were loaded on trucks to the camp. We were assigned to the 33rd Training Battalion.

The army training day began with a bugler playing reveille. At "first call", the platoon sergeant would awaken his troops, have them fall out at attention on platoon formation for roll call, barking, "Report!" Each squad leader in turn would answer, (providing no absentees), "All present and accounted for." When all the sergeants had reported, the 1st Sgt., doing an about face to the company commander reporting, "All present and accounted for Sir." The officer would then dismiss the troops and the soldiers would head for the mess hall for breakfast. After breakfast, in classes of 30 minutes duration, began the training of map and compass reading, firing guns, and taking apart and reassembling the guns and equipment; posting and changing of the guard; how to plot and plant a mine field; long 25 forced march miles in the least amount of time. The gas mask training included entering a building that was filled with tear gas and also sniffing a little of the gas. We also traveled to the rifle range many times until we felt comfortable shooting accurately and quickly. The obstacle course consisted of barbed wire fences with live ammunition falling over our heads, perhaps 8 or 10 feet above. We crawled on our stomachs and crept under the wire many times. We had a firing range where enemy figures of cardboard would bounce up before us as if they were the enemy. We had to be quick and accurate to hit the targets at 100 to 200 yds. out because they were up for only an instance and then out of sight. On the rifle range I qualified for marksmanship and became a sharpshooter at ranges of 200, 300 and 500 yards in the standing, prone, and sitting positions. I also was above average in "rapid fire". I never was an expert. Later, as I became a non-commissioned officer, I had charge of the rifle range pits. We would grade the soldiers at which point there bullets hit the bull's eye. It was a "5" for a bull's eye and downward, each circle was a point less. The targets would be pulled down after each shot, examined and marked by a metal disk on a pole, raised and repositioned so that the score could be marked. A "miss" would be a waving red flag called "Maggie's Drawers". All soldiers had to qualify to be sent overseas. Whether they tried to fail or couldn't shoot straight, we qualified them. They became marksmen. This duty in the pits caused a ringing in my ears that is still with me to this day. We had to learn mounting and dismounting on half-tracks in the shortest amount of time. After practicing, we could mount and dismount in 6 to 8 seconds. Dismounting was easy as you just jumped off, but on mounting a half-track, each individual had a certain part or area of the vehicle to mount, some climbed on the tracks. We simulated attacking and burning buildings. We climbed wooden walls and swung on ropes across water-filled ditches. We had bayonet training, jabbing at hanging bags. We hop-scotched running through rubber tires and crawled through round barrel-like tubes. We were taught a little of the martial arts and also learned the "manual of arms". This procedure was left and right shoulder arms, present arms, port arms, order arms and parade rest. We also had constant close order drills and calisthenics. The "Articles of War" were again read to us to drive home the consequences to us if they were not obeyed. The punishment was severe. The punishment could be K.P., restricted to quarters, or marching on the parade grounds with full field pack for hours. The harshest punishment was the stockade from a court martial or being made to excavate a 6 by 6 foot hole, fill it up and dig it out again. I tell you, It didn't take long before everyone obeyed all orders. If any infraction of rules was not admitted to by the offender, the punishment was for the whole platoon to fall out early in the morning with full field equipment for a 25 mile hike, sometimes at double-time. We soon had a well-oiled bunch of soldiers, well drilled and obeying orders. We were like zombies. But let me tell you this, later on, many lives were saved because of this regimentation. There were many classes to attend, and the soldiers, standing at attention in platoon formation would salute and if armed, would present arms as the bugle sounded retreat as the flag was lowered. The day was over. After supper was served, we were on our own to go to town, post exchange or the day room where many games were played along with reading material if there was no duty like guard duty, kitchen police (KP) or any other duties. At nine o'clock, "Taps" would be played, a sad and mournful sound. Taps was first introduced in the Civil War. One evening, Gen. Daniel Butterfield, humming and whistling some notes, told his bugler to play them. The bugler played and the general liked it. The refrain spread like wild-fire through the army replacing the regulation "Lights out". Taps is used in all military funerals and at the end of a soldier's day. Meals were satisfactory and consisted of chipped beef (S.O.S.), gooey eggs, chili concarne, and chicken on Sunday noon and cold-cuts at night. One time we rebelled so much about chili concarne, we all skipped dinner. They marched us in with loaded guns and we had to take it. All in all it was a great experience. We had been raw recruits, but now we were "smartly" looking soldiers. The thirteen weeks of basic training was over in October and our next camp was Pine Camp (now called Fort Drum, located in upstate New York above Watertown).

This is where we began winter training, sleeping in bedrolls and going on long marches on half-tracks and tanks all over New York State. It was peacetime so we always returned to the barracks, but when war came with Pearl Harbor, we were tented in the field for the duration. In September, 1942 we were on Tennessee maneuvers. We were divided into two groups – the Red Army and the Blue Army to simulate wartime conditions. This included crossing rivers on small rubber boats or riding across on pontoon bridges which we carried to the river's edge. The red clay was terrible and it seemed to rain all of the time. This training really paid off since we now had greater endurance and could be off in a moment's notice.

On about November 17, 1942 we entrained for California – Camp Young or Camp Ibis. Now we trained for desert warfare and to stand the brutal heat in full gear on marches and some-times even wearing gas masks. On many marches, we had many casualties from the heat. We had bayonet training, hand-to-hand combat, martial arts and compass reading.

It was very hard navigating around in the desert because landmarks were hard to identify especially at night, so many times we were lost. No matter where we were in training, there was always the reading of the Articles of War, lectures, calisthenics and close order drill. We were now all very well trained soldiers ready to fight the enemy anywhere in any terrain. From Indio, California we went by troop train to Camp Bowie, Texas. There the regiment was split into battalions. I was a sergeant in the 10th Armored Infantry Battalion. This was June, 1943. Most of this training was a review of all the other training we had been given. On December 20, 1943 we were sent to Camp Myles Standish in Taunton, Massachusetts where we embarked on the ship, the "John Barry" for the trip to England.

We continued reviewing our training until July, 1944. Now it was combat – where you win or you lose!

Chapter XIX

The Soldiers & Officers With Whom I Served

Enlisted Men

Harry Knight - Omaha, Nebraska. A very good soldier who did everything well - always neat and a man who always did his best. A true friend. Was killed in January, 1945 by a stray bullet. A loss I felt very deeply. Claimed he was a hobo in civilian life.

Sanford Holmes - Princeton, Missouri. Very dedicated and never stepped out of line. Learned very quickly and advanced to become a sergeant. Saw his friend killed in the hedgerows in July. Always backing up his men.

Sylvester Manzitto - Omaha, Nebraska. Made corporal. Did only what was necessary. Never rebelling about orders.

Elvin Sleder - Michigan. Took everything in his stride and went along with his duty. Always loved a drink.

Edward Salber - Kansas. Very good soldier - except should not have been in action. Because he was older than the rest, he should not have been drafted.

Johnson - Tennessee. A happy-go-lucky always singing hillbilly songs. Got along with everybody.

Fred Corcoran - Buffalo, N.Y. Very affable good looking young man. Lost his life in the hedgerows. This did hurt.

Donald Durkes - A close friend. Half-track driver. Always ate my cookies from home. Wrote home constantly. Wounded in the Battle of the Bulge.

Paul McAteer - Too young. Battle fatigue sent him back to get readjusted.

Ed Salvi - Long Island, New York. Always said he couldn't see so I ordered him back to Division for reassignment.

John Rossing - A fine replacement for the platoon. Learned quickly and became a sergeant. Good friend of Sanford Holmes.

Cpl. Slavik - Omaha, Nebraska. Was my understudy for a short time.

Noel Chalfant - Ohio. Fought in the hedgerows.

Thomas Carpenter - Newport, Rhode Island. An Army man who was busted many times from the rank of sergeant because of being AWOL and drinking.

Stanley Putzig - of Stamford Connecticut. Very apprehensive. Would help in many ways but not a fighter. Very cautious, but was friendly.

Dom Calvetti - Illinois. Do not remember much of him.

Company Officers

Officers of "A" Company - Capt. Donnely, Capt. Tessier, Lt. Miller

Officers of "C" Company - Capt. Leighton, Lt. Spencer, Lt. Young, Lt. Baum, Lt. Levitt, Lt. Robberts, Lt. Wilson and Lt. Cardella

Sergeants in my "A" Company Platoon - Sgts. Kennedy, Plourde, Pennington, Michalek, Wells, Fratacangelo, Basso
Armand Pollutro was my half-track driver. There were others who served under me, but I cannot recall their names.

After the war I made good friends with Melvirn Mills, John Madden, Patrick Conte, Carmen Basso, Sanford Holmes, John Rossing, Sidney Shapiro, Mathew Grbovac (who was a motor pool Sgt.), and Sgt. Jackson Vail who came home later in January on furlough.

Chapter XX

Awards, Citations, History & Letters Home

History**

The 4th Armored Division was activated, 15th of April, 1941 and trained at Pine Camp, N.Y. In September and October, 1942, the division took part in maneuvers in Tennessee as part of the 2nd Army. Training and maneuvers in the Desert Training Center followed December, 1942 through February, 1943 and April to July 1943. The division then moved to Camp Bowie, Texas for further training before leaving Boston 29th of December for England.

Battle Credits WWII: (Division) Normandy, Northern France, Rhineland, Ardennes, and Central Europe.

Comm. Generals:

    Maj Gen Henry W. Baird Apr '41 to May '42

    Maj Gen John S. Wood May '42 to Dec '44

    Maj Gen Hugh J. Gaffey Dec '44 to Mar '45

    Maj Gen William M. Hoge Mar '45 to Jul '45

    Maj Gen Fay B. Prickett Sep '45 to Inactivation

Combat History: After training in England, Jan-Jul '44, the 4th Armored Division landed at Utah Beach, Jul 11. '44 and entered combat Jul 17, attacking and securing the Coutances Area, Jul 28. The division then moved south and captured Nantes, cutting France north of the Loire, smashed across the Moselle, Sep 11-13, flanked Nancy and to Henamenil, Sep 27 to Oct 11. The division rested briefly before returning in Nov, advanced through Dieuze and crossed the Saar River, the 21st-22nd of Nov to establish and expand the bridgehead and took Singling and Bining before being relieved Dec 8th. Two days after the Germans launched their Ardennes offensive, the 4th Armored entered the fight, 18th of Dec '44 driving Northwest into Belgium, covering 150 miles in 19 hours. The division attacked the Germans at Bastogne, helping to relieve the besieged 101st Airborne. After six weeks of waiting for another German attack, the division jumped off from Luxembourg City in an eastward drive that carried it across the Moselle River at Treis, south and east of Worms, and across the Rhine Mar 24-25, 1945, and continued to push on. Lauterbach fell 29th of Mar, Creuzburg across the Werra River on the 1st of Apr, Gotha on the 4th, and by the 12th of Apr, the division was across the Saale River. Pursuit of the enemy continued and by the 6th of May, the division had crossed into Czechoslovakia, established a bridgehead across the Otara River at Strakonice, with forward elements at Pisek. After a tour of occupational duty, the 4th returned to the U.S. for inactivation, Apr '46.

Honors: Medals of Honor   -Three
                     Distinguished Unit Citation-One; to the
                     entire division

Foreign Awards: One French Fourragere

FROM 4TH ARMORED DIVISION HEADQUARTERS

GENERAL ORDERS NUMBER 70   29 Apr 1945

TO COMMANDING OFFICERS, ALL UNITS AND SEPARATE ORGANIZATIONS 4TH ARMORED DIVISION, AND ALL ATTACHED UNITS

The relief of the 4th Armored Division from the front line follows a long period of sustained offensive combat in which you have distinguished yourselves by an outstanding feat of arms. During the press of battle, it is inevitable that standards of dress and discipline will deteriorate.

It is essential that the high reputation of the 4th Armored Division for discipline and meticulous dress be maintained. The present period offers each member of the division an opportunity to regain those standards of dress and deportment which have been habitual in this command in the past.

The appearance and conduct of our troops of our troops during the static phases of the occupation of

Germany will be closely observed by enemy nationals and this division is expected to set the same standards of leadership in these departments as it has in battle.

It is the responsibility of each officer and non-commissioned officer in this command to establish and maintain these standards at the earliest opportunity.

W. M. Hoge
Brigadier General, U.S. Army
Commanding

FROM 4TH ARMORED DIVISION HEADQUARTERS

GENERAL ORDERS NUMBER 94   28 May 1945

SECTION VII AWARD OF OAK-LEAF CLUSTER TO PURPLE HEART MEDAL

Under the provisions of AR 600-45, 22 September 1943, as amended, in addition to the Purple Heart Medal previously awarded, a bronze Oak-Leaf Cluster is awarded to the following for wounds received in action against the enemy.

To Corporal *RALPH ADKINS* 35775254 FA, 1945 Germany. Entered military service from Kentucky.

To Sergeant *CHARLES G. ANGELINA* 33075391 Ord, 1944, France. Entered military service from Pennsylvania.

To Staff Sergeant *WALTER FLEISCHMAN* 32215156 Armd, 1945, Belgium. Entered military service from New York.

To Sergeant *GEORGE W. HALLDEN, JR* 35289056 Armd, 1944, France. Entered military service from Ohio.

To Private First Class *FRANK J. SUARINO* 32091722
Armd, 1945, Germany. Entered military service from
New York.

To First Lieutenant *EMERT W. LINDROOS* 02010568
Cav, 1945, Germany. Entered military service from
Idaho.

To Technical Sergeant *EUGENE W. LUCIANO*
31048909 Inf, 1944, France. Entered military service
from Connecticut.

To Technician Fourth Grade *ELMER R. SMITH*
33081555 Inf, 1944, Germany. Entered military service from Pennsylvania.

To Private First Class *SAM CAPRI* 336112744 MD,
1945, Belgium. Entered military service from Pennsylvania.

To Technician Fifth Grade *ROBERT E. MILTON*
20703365 Inf, 1945, Germany. Entered military service from Iowa.

BY COMMAND OF
MAJOR GENERAL WILLIAM M. HOGE

** Source: 4th Armored Division Records, Maps and
Casualties

Letters Home

A chilly afternoon
somewhere in France
Thursday, Nov. 2, 1944

Dear Mom and Dad,

As the skies put on their coat of gray, and the silver clouds go drifting on their way and the trees have changed the green attire to the brilliance of rainbows everywhere, it brings back the memories of those autumn days of New England, when we could enjoy the pleasures and pastimes known, as it seems, to that part of the world. Although it is nice to reminice of those beautiful times, I wouldn't leave here under any circumstance until this job is cleared up so the danger of leaving home is very remote. I wonder if the old town is like it used to be, but I don't believe it could with so many of the boys away. The girls must be having hard times in the old town, but I can assure you a big change will take place as soon as the boys get back... anyway marriages will be many.

Up to this day, I haven't heard from Arthur or Irene I've told you previously when I have seen them both.

I am looking forward to a Christmas and I'll still be looking. But what is the difference, any day will be Christmas when this is settled.

Your Son,
Gene

Kelheim, Germany
On the Danube
8 June 1945

Dear Folks:

As the blue Danube rolls east to the sea, I expect very soon to travel west over seas. I have been hoping that maybe tomorrow or even the next day I can start on my way but until the time comes to go, I'll still be here along the Danube where it flows through the town of Kelheim which is 50 miles north of Munich, about 100 miles from the Swiss border and 12 miles from Regensburg. I do not think you can find the locality of Kelheim on the map, but you will find the general whereabouts of it. This is a large factory area with slave labor barracks attached to it. It never has been touched by Allied bombing. The slave labor barracks were a shambles when we first came here, ,but they are in pretty fair shape now. The cockroaches and bedbugs are all over these rooms, even though we fumigated the place. We don't have any beds, but sleep on the floor.

In fact, there must have been a lot of Italian prisoners here because there is Italian writings all over our lockers, etc. My room isn't half bad with painted walls, a new ceiling, a new floor and all the necessary equipment for an office.

The boys fixed up the courtyard between the 4 buildings which are in a square. It looks swell compared to what it was. The lister bag (drinking water)

Front row, Left to right: Leo Dwyer, Gene Luciano, Joseph Noel, Wilkens, Walter Betchel, Theodore Ray, Frank Fedus, Cook, Stuart Stott, Adrian Tessier, Lt. Abe Baum, Lt. Levitt, Capt. Leighton, Lt. Young, Lt. Spencer, Edward Osmanski, George Nelson, James Watt, Edward Kreuzer, Alfred Mancini, James Hoy, Thomas Winebarger, Jackson Vail, Ralph Sorrell, Richard Manning.

JOHN W. GIRTON
Captain
Commanding

GEORGE D. SMITH
First Lieutenant

JAMES C. THOMPSON
Second Lieutenant

ROBERT R. VOLTZ
Second Lieutenant

COMPANY F

★

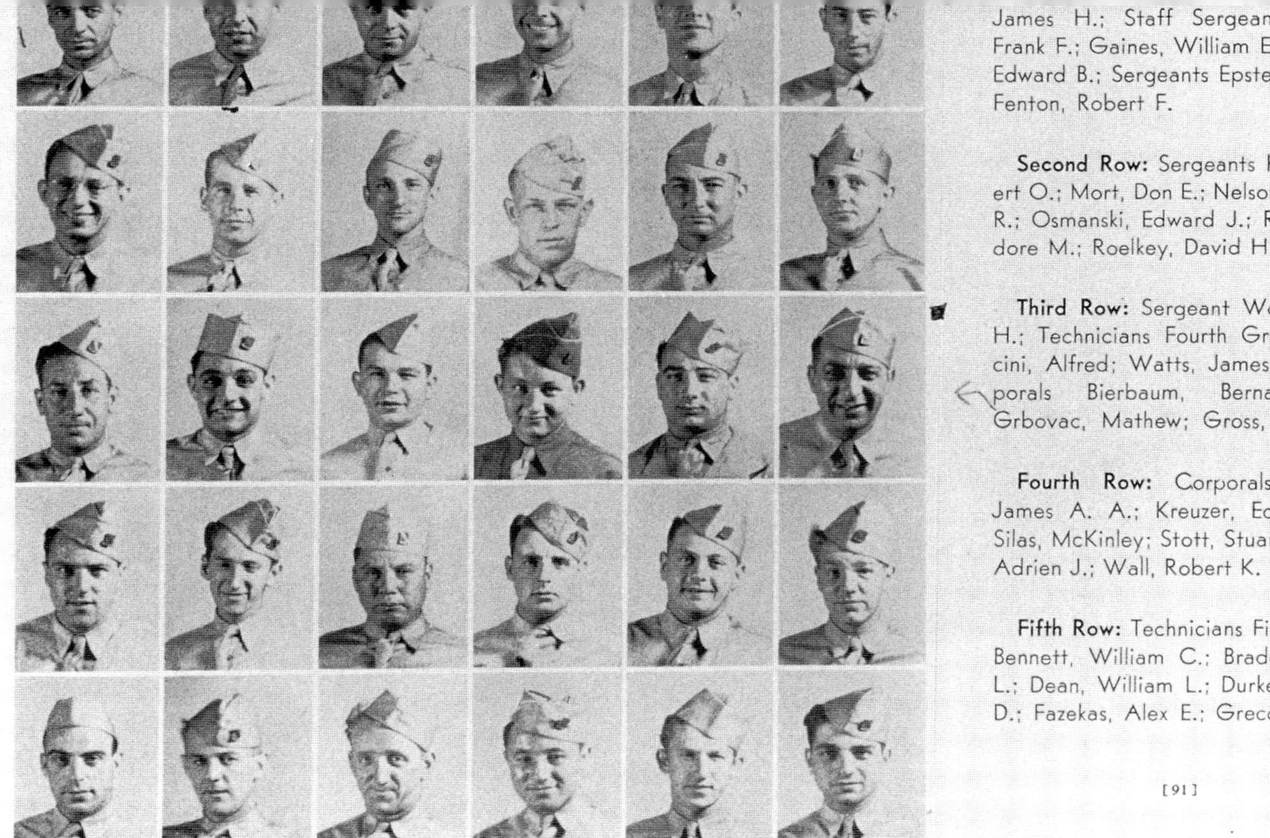

James H.; Staff Sergeants Fedus, Frank F.; Gaines, William E.; Lawson, Edward B.; Sergeants Epstein, Harry; Fenton, Robert F.

Second Row: Sergeants Kutz, Robert O.; Mort, Don E.; Nelson, George R.; Osmanski, Edward J.; Ray, Theodore M.; Roelkey, David H.

Third Row: Sergeant Wood, John H.; Technicians Fourth Grade Mancini, Alfred; Watts, James G.; Corporals Bierbaum, Bernard M.; Grbovac, Mathew; Gross, Sigmund.

Fourth Row: Corporals Jeffrey, James A. A.; Kreuzer, Edward O.; Silas, McKinley; Stott, Stuart; Tessier, Adrien J.; Wall, Robert K.

Fifth Row: Technicians Fifth Grade Bennett, William C.; Braden, Derrill L.; Dean, William L.; Durkes, Donald D.; Fazekas, Alex E.; Greco, Sam A.

COMPANY F

(Reading from Left to Right)

First Row: Technicians Fifth Grade Hardman, Carl I.; Huffman, Robert N.; Kondash, Michael; McCullough, Leonard; Morris, James T.; Painter, Norman H.

Second Row: Technicians Fifth Grade Penzone, Anthony; Quenzer, Edward L.; Riggio, Anthony C.; Riley, Clyde M.; Rowe, Clifford E.; Sacco, Joseph, Jr.; Spencer, Carlton M.

Third Row: Technicians Fifth Grade Spencer, Carlton, M.; Wilkins, James D.; Privates First Class Blackburn, Arthur E.; Bodnar, Joseph; Catlin, Elmer L.

Fourth Row: Privates First Class Chalfant, Noel B.; Christopher, Atlee R.; Cooke, Thomas E.; Dabek, Ollie J.; Davidson, Robert R.; Dolce, Michael J.

Fifth Row: Privates First Class Drella, Sigmund A.; Dwyer, Leo M.; Fenik, George S.; Frank, Ben; Henzler, Albert D. C.; Hoy, James W.

Sixth Row: Privates First Class Janas, Adam J.; Kelley, Hardy; Kindt, Bernard O.; Kronenbitter, Charles

Leinaweaver, John E.; Lewandowski, Clement L.; Lucey, Howard J.; Manning, Richard F.

Eighth Row: Privates First Class McAdams, James B.; McClung, Oland A.; Mills, Melvin E.; Montell, John J.; Myers, Leroy J.; Nagy, Paul.

Ninth Row: Privates First Class Noel, Joseph L.; Pollace, Jack V.; Rzonca, Stanley; Sacchetti, Richard J.; Scarpa, Anthony J.; Seeley, Clayton L.

Tenth Row: Privates First Class Shato, Henry L.; Thompson, Robert J.; Vail, Jackson B.; Wicks, Joseph; Privates Adams, Lee M. Brown, William G.

★

MEN WHOSE PHOTOGRAPHS DO NOT APPEAR IN THIS BOOK

Staff Sergeant Causey, John J.; Technician Fifth Grade Sharp, John F., Jr.; Privates First Class Bartos, George J.; Keane, William H.; Kent, Willis E.; Loftus, William J.; Privates Brown, Robert J.; Carpenter, James H.; Ford, Bert F.; Hager, Robert F.; Johancen, John J.; Juaraz, Robert E.; Manlitto, Silvester.

COMPANY F

(Reading from Left to Right)

First Row: Privates Colledge, David J.; Collier, Elmer L.; Daddi, Joseph; DeRose, Ralph; Dibert, Evan M.; Dubec, Frank A.

Second Row: Privates Hill, Henry C.; Hofferer, Carl J.; Hogya, Joseph; Janecke, Louis R.; Jewell, Harold E.; Kelley, Raphael J.

Third Row: Privates Knight, Harry F.; Kochanski, Peter J.; Kreider, Milton R.; Kruse, Earlyon J.; Kupres, Joseph; Lampert, Charles, Jr.

Fourth Row: Privates Langenberg, Harry E.; Leinart, Donald L.; Liggett, Harold L.; Luciano, Eugene W.; Malloy, Edward V.; Marshall, Edward F.

Fifth Row: Privates Matson, Vernon L.; McCarrell, Wallance E.; McCullough, Harold B.; McWilliams, Henry G.; Meinke, Frederick A.; Modin, Lyle W.

Sixth Row: Privates Mollicone, Joseph; Nelson, Leroy F.; Oakley, Hu-

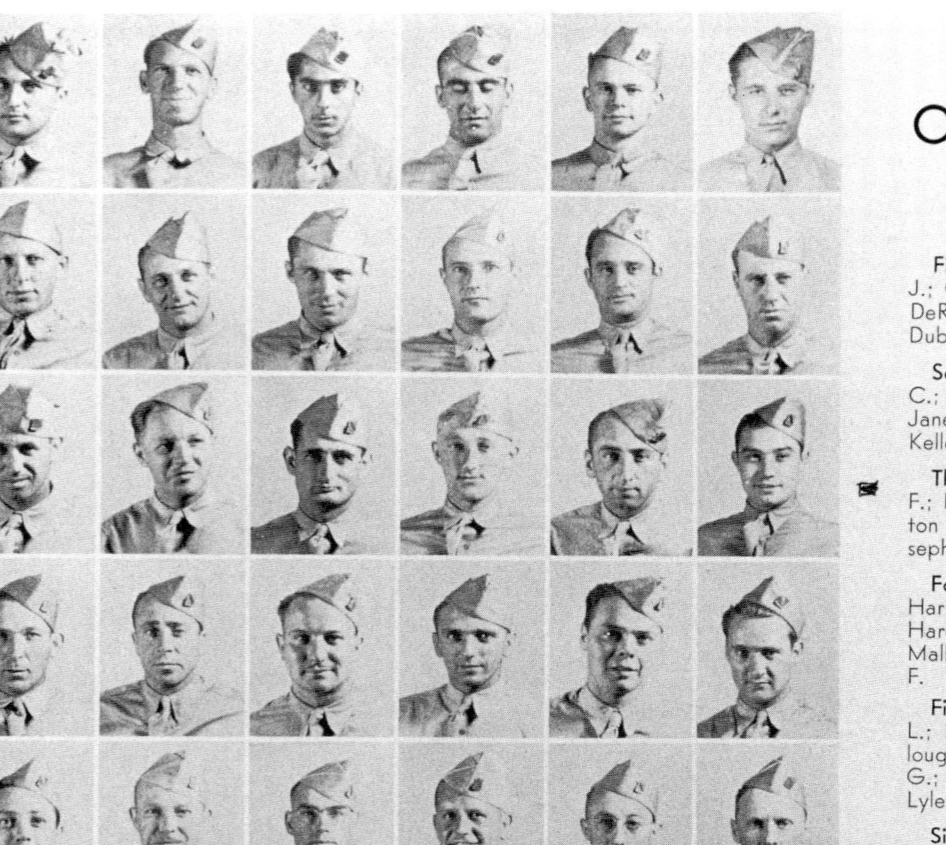

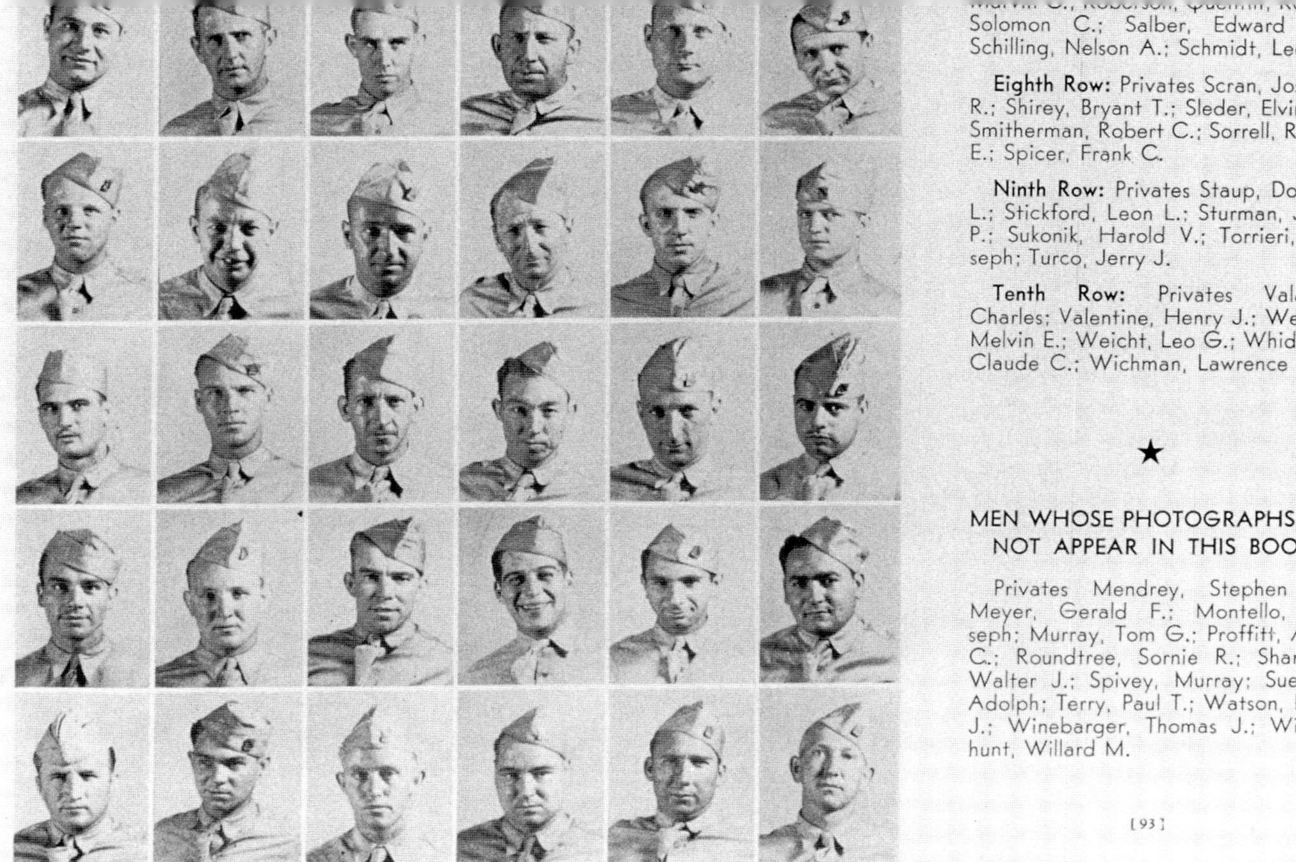

Marvin C.; Roberson, Quentin, Royal, Solomon C.; Salber, Edward H.; Schilling, Nelson A.; Schmidt, Leo C.

Eighth Row: Privates Scran, Joseph R.; Shirey, Bryant T.; Sleder, Elvin E.; Smitherman, Robert C.; Sorrell, Ralph E.; Spicer, Frank C.

Ninth Row: Privates Staup, Donald L.; Stickford, Leon L.; Sturman, John P.; Sukonik, Harold V.; Torrieri, Joseph; Turco, Jerry J.

Tenth Row: Privates Valasck, Charles; Valentine, Henry J.; Weber, Melvin E.; Weicht, Leo G.; Whidden, Claude C.; Wichman, Lawrence F.

★

MEN WHOSE PHOTOGRAPHS DO NOT APPEAR IN THIS BOOK

Privates Mendrey, Stephen R.; Meyer, Gerald F.; Montello, Joseph; Murray, Tom G.; Proffitt, Arlie C.; Roundtree, Sornie R.; Sharkey, Walter J.; Spivey, Murray; Suelter, Adolph; Terry, Paul T.; Watson, Fred J.; Winebarger, Thomas J.; Wisenhunt, Willard M.

[93]

Army of the United States

SEPARATION QUALIFICATION RECORD

SAVE THIS FORM IT WILL NOT BE REPLACED IF LOST

This record of job assignments and special training received in the Army is furnished to the soldier when he leaves the service. In its preparation information is taken from available Army records and supplemented by personal interview. The information about civilian education and work experience is based on the individual's own statements. The veteran may present this document to former employers, prospective employers, representatives of schools or colleges, or use it in any other way that may prove beneficial to him.

1. LAST NAME FIRST NAME MIDDLE INITIAL			MILITARY OCCUPATIONAL ASSIGNMENTS		
LUCIANO, EUGENE V			10. MONTHS	11. GRADE	12. MILITARY OCCUPATIONAL SPECIALTY
2. ARMY SERIAL NO	3. GRADE	4. SOCIAL SECURITY NO	3	Pvt	Basic Training 521
31048909	T/Sgt	Unknown	48	T/Sgt	Platoon Sergeant 745
5. PERMANENT MAILING ADDRESS (Street/City, County, State)					
237 East Main St					
Torrington (Litchfield) Conn					
6. DATE OF ENTRY INTO ACTIVE SERVICE	7. DATE OF SEPARATION	8. DATE OF BIRTH			
9 July 41	24 Oct 45	30 Apr 16			
9. PLACE OF SEPARATION					
Fort Devens Mass					

SUMMARY OF MILITARY OCCUPATIONS

13. TITLE—DESCRIPTION—RELATED CIVILIAN OCCUPATION

PLATOON SERGEANT: Was in charge of a rifle platoon of armored infantry. Was responsib
for fifty-five men and five half-track vehicles. Supervised the fighting and
defensive tactics of the platoon. Worked in coordination with the 4th Armored Division
in France, Belgium, and Germany.

Army of the United States

Honorable Discharge

This is to certify that

EUGENE V LUCIANO 31 048 909 TECHNICAL SERGEANT.

Company C 27th Armored Infantry Battalion

Army of the United States

*is hereby Honorably Discharged from the military
service of the United States of America.*

*This certificate is awarded as a testimonial of Honest
and Faithful Service to this country.*

Given at   Separation Center
Fort Devens Mass

Date   24 October 1945

C W OATLEY
Major AGD

CONPANY :A: TENTH ARMORED INFANTRY BATTALION
A.P.O. 254 , U.S. Army

4 May 1945

SUBJECT: Certificate of Merit.

TO   Commanding Officer, 10th Arm'd Inf. Bn.,
        A.P.O. 254, U. S. Army.

    1. It is recommended that T/Sgt. Eugene W. Luciano, 31048909,
this company be awarded the Certificate of Merit. The following
facts serve as a basis for this recommendation:

    a. T/Sgt. Eugene W. Luciano has carried out the duties of
both Squd Leader and Platoon Sergeant in this battalion in a manner
which is praiseworthy.

    b. T/Sgt. Luciano has always been known to have the most
efficient and best organized platoon in his company due to his expert
leardership and devotion to duty. Twice he has been called upon to
take over his platoon in combat, due to the loss of a platoon leader,
and has done in a manner to be proud of.

    c. T/Sgt. Luciano, over a long period of time, has performed
his duties in a manner which indicates a high standard of personal
responsibility and unit pride.

                                    _____ J. MCNELLY,
                            1st Lt., 10th Armd. Inf. Bn.
                            Commanding.

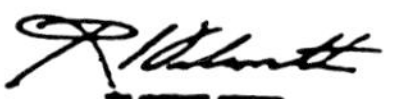

DEPARTMENT OF THE ARMY
THIS IS TO CERTIFY THAT THE SECRETARY OF THE ARMY HAS AWARDED
THE ARMY COMMENDATION MEDAL
TO   TECHNICAL SERGEANT ROGER L. LUCIANO, UNITED STATES ARMY
FOR   conspicuously meritorious and outstanding performance of military duty in
France, Belgium, Luxembourg and Germany from July 17, 1944 to May 4, 1945.
GIVEN UNDER MY HAND IN THE CITY OF WASHINGTON
THIS   16th   DAY OF September   19 54

EUROPEAN THEATER OF OPERATIONS — UNITED STATES ARMY
HEADQUARTERS FOURTH
ARMORED DIVISION
CERTIFICATE OF MERIT
is awarded to
Technical Sergeant Roger L. Luciano 1st—8919 Infantry
ARMORED DIV
IN RECOGNITION OF CONSPICUOUSLY MERITORIOUS AND OUTSTANDING PERFORMANCE
OF MILITARY DUTY
Citation
MAJOR GENERAL US ARMY
COMMANDING

THE UNITED STATES OF AMERICA

TO ALL WHO SHALL SEE THESE PRESENTS, GREETING:

THIS IS TO CERTIFY THAT
THE PRESIDENT OF THE UNITED STATES OF AMERICA
HAS AWARDED THE

PURPLE HEART

ESTABLISHED BY GENERAL GEORGE WASHINGTON
AT NEWBURGH, NEW YORK, AUGUST 7, 1782
TO

TECHNICAL SERGEANT EUGENE V. LUCIANO, UNITED STATES ARMY

FOR WOUNDS RECEIVED
IN ACTION
European Theater 26 September 19--
GIVEN UNDER MY HAND IN THE CITY OF WASHINGTON
THIS 26 DAY OF June 19 86

THE UNITED STATES OF AMERICA

TO ALL WHO SHALL SEE THESE PRESENTS, GREETING: THIS IS TO CERTIFY THAT THE PRESIDENT
OF THE UNITED STATES OF AMERICA AUTHORIZED BY EXECUTIVE ORDER, 24 AUGUST 1962 HAS AWARDED

THE BRONZE STAR MEDAL

TO   TECHNICAL SERGEANT EUGENE W. LUCIANO, UNITED STATES ARMY

FOR   meritorious achievement in ground combat against the armed
enemy during world war II in the European-African-Middle
Eastern Theater of Operations.

GIVEN UNDER MY HAND IN THE CITY OF WASHINGTON
THIS 4th DAY OF June 19 86

WESTERN UNION

A. N. WILLIAMS
PRESIDENT

1201

The filing time shown in the date line on telegrams and day letters is STANDARD TIME at point of origin. Time of receipt is STANDARD TIME at point of destination

NAU #! GOVT=WUX WASHINGTON DC 17 401A

ANTONIO LUCIANO=

237 EAST MAIN ST. TORRINGTON CONN=

REGRET TO INFORM YOU YOUR SON STAFF SERGEANT EUGENE W
LUCIANO WAS SLIGHTLY WOUNDED IN ACTION TWENTY FIVE NOVEMBER
IN FRANCE YOU WILL BE ADVISED AS REPORTS OF CONDITION ARE
RECEIVED=

DUNLOP ACTING THE ADJUTANT GENERAL.

WESTERN UNION

A. N. WILLIAMS
PRESIDENT

1201

CLASS OF SERVICE

This is a full-rate Telegram or Cablegram unless its deferred character is indicated by a suitable symbol above or preceding the address.

SYMBOLS

DL – Day Letter

NL – Night Letter

LC – Deferred Cable

NLT – Cable Night Letter

Ship Radiogram

(50)

1945 JAN 12

The filing time shown in the date line on telegrams and day letters is STANDARD TIME at point of origin.   Time of receipt is STANDARD TIME at point of destination.

NAU156 7 AREA SIX FCAMPSHANKS NY 12 526P

MR AND MRS A LUCIANO=

237 EASTMAIN ST TORRINGTON CONN=.

ARRIVED NY SAFELY HOME IN FEW DAYS=
GENE.

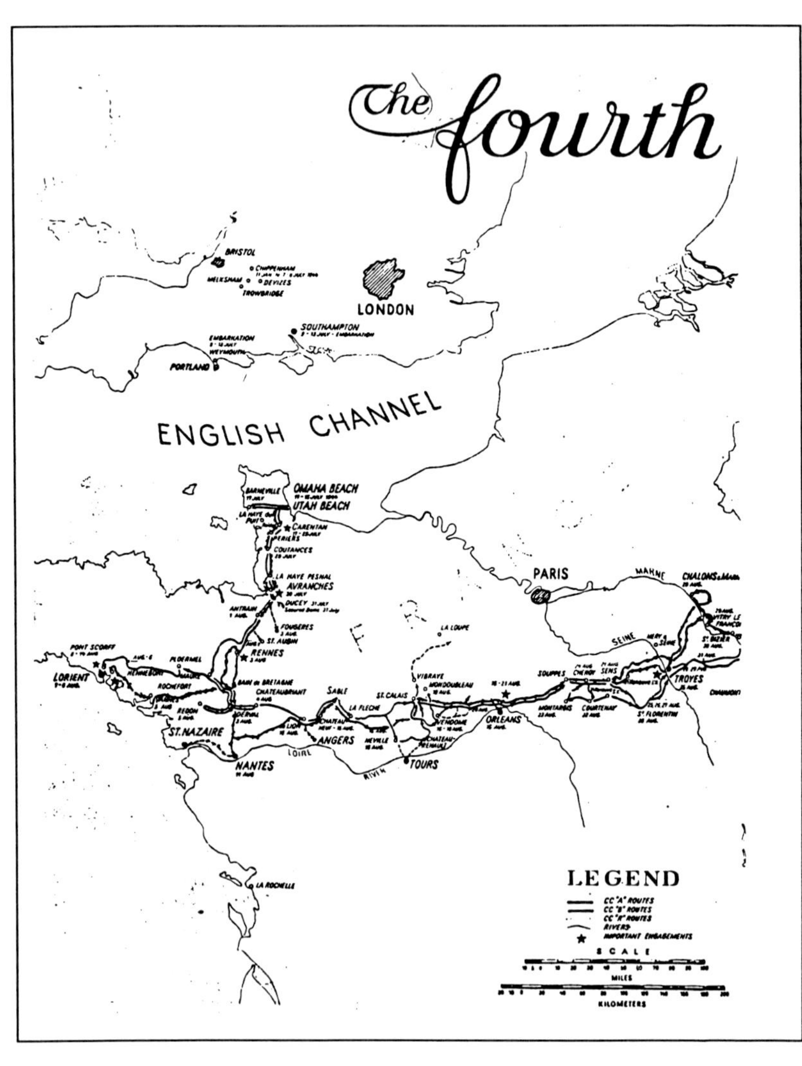
The fourth
BRISTOL
CHIPPENHAM
MELKSHAM
DEVIZES
TROWBRIDGE
LONDON
SOUTHAMPTON
EMBARKATION
WEYMOUTH
PORTLAND
ENGLISH CHANNEL
BARNEVILLE
OMAHA BEACH
UTAH BEACH
LA HAYE du PUITS
CARENTAN
PERIERS
COUTANCES
LA HAYE PESNAL
AVRANCHES
DUCEY
ANTRAIN
ST. AUBIN
FOUGERES
PONT SCORFF
RENNES
PLOERMEL
LORIENT
HENNEBONT
ROCHEFORT
BAIN de BRETAGNE
CHATEAUBRIANT
SABLE
ST. CALAIS
VIBRAYE
MONDOUBLEAU
SOUPPES
CHENOY
SENS
PARIS
MARNE
CHALONS s MARN
SEINE
ST. DIZER
VITRY LE FRANCOI
TROYES
CHAUMONT
LA LOUPE
REDON
JOSNAL
LA FLECHE
NANTES
ST. NAZAIRE
ANGERS
NEVILLE
CHATEAU-
RENAUL
ORLEANS
MONTARGIS
COURTENAY
ST. FLORENTIN
LOIRE
TOURS
VENDOME
LA ROCHELLE
LEGEND
CC "A" ROUTES
CC "B" ROUTES
CC "R" ROUTES
RIVERS
IMPORTANT ENGAGEMENTS
SCALE
MILES
KILOMETERS

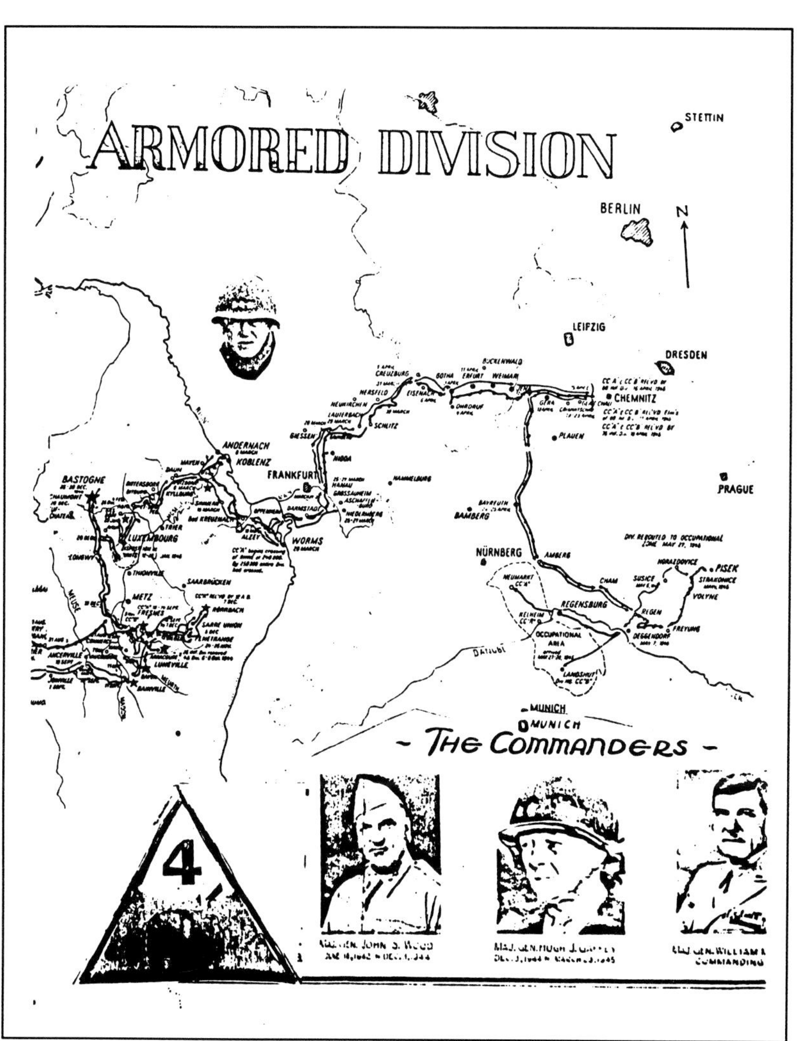
ARMORED DIVISION
- THE COMMANDERS -
STETTIN
BERLIN
N
LEIFZIG
DRESDEN
BUCHENWALD
CREUZBURG
GOTHA ERFURT WEIMAR
MERSFELD EISENACH
CHEMNITZ
NEUKIRCHEN
LAUTERBACH
SCHLITZ
GIESSEN
ANDERNACH
KOBLENZ
FRANKFURT
HANAU
GROSSAUHEIM ASCHAFFEN
HAMMELBURG
PLAUEN
PRAGUE
BASTOGNE
TRIER
LUXEMBOURG
ALZEY
WORMS
BAD KREUZNACH
OFFENBEIM
DARMSTADT
BAYREUTH
BAMBERG
NÜRNBERG
AMBERG
REGENSBURG
NEUMARKT
CC "A"
KELHEIM
CC "B"
OCCUPATIONAL
AREA
LANDSHUT
SAARBRÜCKEN
METZ
ROHRBACH
SAARE UNION
THIONVILLE
LUNEVILLE
CHAM
SUSICE
HORAZDOVICE
PISEK
STRAKONICE
VOLYNE
REGEN
DEGGENDORF
FREYUNG
MUNICH
MAJ. GEN. JOHN S. WOOD
MAJ. GEN. HUGH J. GAFFEY
LT. GEN. WILLIAM M.
COMMANDING

RÉPUBLIQUE FRANÇAISE

Guerre 1939-1945

CITATION

DÉCISION N° 270

LE PRÉSIDENT DU GOUVERNEMENT PROVISOIRE DE LA RÉPUBLIQUE,

CITÉ A L'ORDRE DE L'ARMÉE

....

10th Armored Infantry Battalion

....

"Magnifique Unité possédant les plus hautes vertus militaires.

Au cours de combats acharnés du 27 juillet au 30 juillet 1944 rompt la défense Allemande et s'empare de COUTANCES puis de la position clef d'Avranches

Exploitant immédiatement la percée par une manoeuvre d'une grande audace s'engage dans la brèche sur les arrières ennemis .

En moins de dix jours surmontant avec décision les contre attaques Allemandes elle libère RENNES, VANNES et NANTES et enferme l'ennemi dans LORIENT poursuivant son avance sur un front de 300 Kms elle atteint la Loire et s'empare de NANTES le 11 Août.

Son action foudroyante contribua pour une large part au succès de la Campagne de FRANCE"

Cette citation comporte l'attribution de la Croix de Guerre avec Palme

PARIS, le 22 juillet 1946
Signé : BIDAULT

- EXTRAIT CERTIFIE CONFORME -
PARIS, le 12 DEC 1983
Pour le Ministre et par autorisation
Le Chef du Bureau des Décorations

J.P GROSSO

RÉPUBLIQUE FRANÇAISE

Guerre 1939-1945

CITATION

DÉCISION N° 271

LE PRÉSIDENT DU GOUVERNEMENT PROVISOIRE DE LA RÉPUBLIQUE ;

CITÉ A L'ORDRE DE L'ARMÉE

....

10th Armored Infantry Battalion

....

"Splendide Unité animée d'une énergie farouche, qui a déjà fait ses preuves en NORMANDIE.

Du 12 au 29 Septembre 1944, précédant l'avance de la IIIe Armée à travers la MOSELLE, s'est emparée de plusieurs positions clefs et a infligé des pertes considérables à l'ennemi.

Par ses actions audacieuses et agressives a largement contribué au succès des Armées Alliées qui repoussèrent l'ennemi hors de FRANCE".

Cette citation comporte l'attribution de la Croix de Guerre avec Palme.

PARIS, le 22 juillet 1946

Signé : BIDAULT

- EXTRAIT CERTIFIE CONFORME -

PARIS, le 12 DEC 1983
Pour le Ministre et par autorisation
Le Chef du Bureau des Décorations

J.P GROSSO

RÉPUBLIQUE FRANÇAISE

Guerre 1939-1945

CITATION

DÉCISION N° 272

LE PRÉSIDENT DU GOUVERNEMENT PROVISOIRE DE LA RÉPUBLIQUE,

VU la Décision N° 270 du 22 juillet 1946 attribuant une citation à l'ordre de l'Armée aux Unités de la 4e Armored Division

VU la Décision N° 271 du 22 juillet 1946 attribuant une citation à l'ordre de l'Armée aux Unités de la 4e Armored Division

D E C I D E

Les Unités Américaines appartenant à la 4e Armored Division suivantes :

....

10th Armored Infantry Battalion

....

sont autorisés à porter la fourragère aux couleurs de la Croix de Guerre 1939-1945

PARIS, le 22 juillet 1946

Signé : BIDAULT

- EXTRAIT CERTIFIE CONFORME -
PARIS, le 12 DEC 1983

Pour le Ministre et par autorisation
Le Chef du Bureau des Décorations

J.P GROSSO

is in the center of it with a large sun umbrella over it. There is a nice 4 x 4 fence all around the walks leading up to the water. The walks are filled with gravel. Then we have trees lined up along the edges, and it certainly is nice now.

If I have films, I will take a shot of the place so you can see it. Chow has not been enough lately. The men have to do quite a little patroling for occupational work. Pollutro went to Paris for 7 days to see the place.

There isn't much more to say and I'm rushing this letter because I'm on duty hours writing it. Regards to all.

Your Son,

Gene

P.S. Love to Jo-Ann

Monday, June 18, 1945

Dear Folks:

Your letter dated June 11 arrived today. Fast time for a three cent stamped letter. You don't have to send air-mail anymore. They come pretty fast now. I'm glad you liked the pictures I sent you. Right now I'm in charge of 646 S.S. men and I'm giving them some of their own medicine they once handed out back to them. When I tell them to do something or want something, they do it in a hurry. I don't fool with them and I don't intend to. I have my platoon with me and I pass down the law to them. There is approximately 2000 prisoners taken care of by our company and they snap to attention, click their heels and salute when I pass by; Germans, Hungarians and White-Russians.

Today speaking to a red headed interpreter telling I wanted all ammo, weapons, knives, brought to me in a pile which I finally received and took away. The interpreter thought that I was kidding, so when I told them I'll cut off their food for a couple days, he got humming. And also another way is to tell them, I'll turn them over to the Russians. They say they are bloody and would rather face the firing squad. Some of the prisoners line up near the P.W. cage gate hoping to go on detail so they will get a large meal to eat. They are begging.

One of the Hungarian soldiers drew a picture of Adeline today. Pretty good resemblance. Let me know how long it takes for these letters I send home so I can tell whether to cut out air-mail. I hate V-mail.

Regards to everyone. Irene C. wrote and said she is going home. I believe she has already arrived in the states, because I just received her letter today. Please do not take too much stock in that present for Jo-Ann. It is hardly nothing. I'm trying to get something better.

Your Son,

Gene

Luciano's Pay Scale

At Fort Devens through $21.00/month
Camp Croft-Basic Training

At Fort Drum (then Pine Camp) $30.00/month

Private First Class $36.00/month
(which I never had)

Corporal $42.00/month

Sergeant in the Mojave Desert $84.00/month

Staff Sergeant $96.00/month
(at the end of Desert Training)

Technical Sergeant in England $114.00/month

With Combat Pay $151.00/month

Chapter XXI

Return to Camps –
50 Years Later

Fifty years later, I made a few return visits to different places where I served in the army. There isn't any more Camp Croft. Most of the town's people don't remember it. The little theater is still there. The area is a housing development and a golf course. The city of Spartanburg is so changed that I didn't recognize it. Cleveland Park is still there and the statue of General Dan Morgan was moved from the center to another area.

At Pine Camp, returning with Matthew Grbovac and also later with many other buddies, the place where we billeted were very run down. The mattresses, floors and walls were a mess. Garbage was strewn all over the grounds. The barracks were in horrible condition and were to be demolished. I met some of the National Guard from the western part of New York State. They belonged to the 10th Mountain Division. There is a new area now for the post. Watertown has changed from our times. After 50 years returning with our ladies, and Grbovac, Noel, Mills, Chalfont, Stickford, Janas, and I say, "So long" to this part of our lives. Recently, a gathering of 4th Arm'd soldiers made a pilgrimage to the camp for the dedication of a flagpole to honor the 4th Arm'd Division.

At all of our reunions, it's always a pleasure to attend. We talk of our past experiences and reminders. The commraderie and the warmth of being with the men who shared the same perilous times, will never be forgotten.

In closing, from these memoirs:

Heavenly Father, we implore you to grant your special graces to all the soldiers of the 4th Arm'd Division.

And may their lives, by your guidance, be the shrine of peace, purity, love, labor, understanding & faith.

We beg you, dear Father, to protect and bless them all; and remembering the 1519 4th Arm'd Division soldiers who gave their lives in battle and others who have recently been called to rest in eternal peace, Amen.

Chapter XXII

Final Thoughts

The 4th Arm'd Division's five battle campaigns were, Normandy, Northern France, Rhineland, Ardennes, and Central Europe. The greatest conflicts were in Normandy, Alsace Lorraine, and the Ardennes. The Troyes, Arracourt, and Luneville battles and the relieving and breaking through to Bastogne were with great cost of men and supplies of the division. If Patton was allowed to continue in the Lorraine Campaign and crossed the Rhine River in December 1944, the war would probably have ended by Christmas. The Germans, because of this letup, had an opportunity to regroup in a different area which was in Germany East of the Ardennes. Previously, they were stopped cold in their attempt of a breakthrough towards and through Nancy. Where was our intelligence? What were the Supreme headquarters doing? When Gen. Troy Middleton who was worried and concerned, made the comment, that he had too few troops to hold the Ardennes line, he received a reply from Supreme Headquarters and Gen. Bradley. Why did they say, "Don't worry, the Germans wouldn't be coming there." Did they think the fighting was over? Why didn't they continue pressing the attack to a finish instead of stalemating all our forces? The forces that held that stretch in the Ardennes should have been battle tested soldiers until those "Green" troops of the four divisions, especially the 106th Infantry Division that were holding the line, acquired fighting experience. Why did Eisenhower over-rule Patton's request to cut off the Bastogne area by driving east of the Ardennes. This would have resulted in the capture of all enemy forces in the area. Was it because Eisenhower did not want to give more glory to Patton?

The great recuperative power of the material and supplies coming from the United States to sustain the troops was one reason of us winning the war. The Germans could not replace their losses with the same abundance as the Americans. If the Germans in their attack in the Ardennes could have reached our gas and supply depots, the war would probably have lasted much longer and perhaps it would have been a negotiated peace rather than an unconditional surrender by Germany. Thank God it never happened! The cost of this great war, besides the great loss of life, was the result that ruined England economically and also as a world power. The politicians gave away so much to aid the losers to solvency, that they finally outstripped us in the world markets. The war was a staggering blow to our economy and national debt. We became a debtor nation which we are now slowly recovering from in the 1990's.

Did we really win the war? Yes, we won the war on the battlefield and tried and convicted those of whom were responsible and committed those inhuman atrocities of killing innocent people and raping countries.

Lastly, let me say, that German soldiers were brave fighting men and they were drafted like we were to serve their country. Did they have an alternative? They did not, but they were patriotic to their country. The ones that are to blame, were the evil leaders, and the crooked politicians who led their country down the path into war, causing such atrocities and human suffering. To all the soldiers who gave their lives, along with the enemy, may they rest in peace.

CHAPTER XXIII

CASUALTIES

4TH ARM'D HQ. CO. K.I.A.

ARMSTRONG, LEONARD M.	TEC 5	INF
CONNOLLY, WALTER F.	TEC 5	INF
DARBY, JOHN T.	TEC 5	AMD
FAGANO, CHARLES A.	PVT	INF
FISHER, RALPH B.	TEC 5	INF
FRIEDMAN HOWARD J.	MAJ	CAV
HRITZ, JOHN J.	TEC 5	FA
KOOK, JOSEPH E.	TEC 5	FA
LE MOINE, EUGENE J.	T/SGT	INF
MROZINSKI, THEO A.	T/SGT	INF
O'NEIL, JEREMIAH H.	CPL	INF
OPALIC, NICHOLAS	CAP	INF
ORR, GEORGE E.	TEC 4	INF
SEPEL, JOHN D.	PVT	INF
SILVESTRO, PETER J.	PVT	INF
SLOBOGIN, ROLAND	PVT	INF
SPRAGG, CARL S.	1 LT	CAV

4 AD COM COMMAND A

BOUWMAN, EDWARD J.	TEC 5	INF
MAHERS, GEORGE C;	TEC 5	AMD
MARCUS, STANLEY S.	TEC 4	INF

| MATHES, HAROLD A. | PVT | AMD |
| SHEPARDSON, LEN H. | TEC 5 | INF |

4 AD COM COMMAND B

ALBRIGHT, BRINTON S.	S/SGT	INF
BRUSS, MICHAEL	TEC 5	INF
OLSON, ARTHUR G.	1 LT	CAV

4 A DIVISION HQ RES COMMD

| STORCK, LOUIS J. | COL | INF |

144TH ARMD SIG CO

| MILLER, WILLIAM R. | PVT | SC |
| POWELL, WILLIAM O. | PFC | SC |

126TH ORD MAINT CO

DOYLE, JAMES E.	PVT	ORD
HARMYCH, MICHAEL NMI	TEC 4	ORD
HELMCAMP, THOMAS, JR	PVT	ORD
JANSON, CLAYTON E.	PFC	ORD
JOHANNSEN, GERALD H.	PVT	ORD
JOYCE, RICHARD J.	TEC 5	ORD
KINYON, LLOYD E.	1 LT	ORD
LAWRENCE, JOSEPH B.	T/SGT	ORD
MACKENZIE, JOHN E.	TEC 5	ORD

4TH ARMD PLAT

| MC KAY, ALBERT | PVT | MP |
| MENKELLO, GEORGE W. | PVT | MP |

10TH ARMD INF BN

ABEL, LESTER C.	PVT	INF
ALTAMIRANO, PETE B.	PVT	INF
ANGUS, LYNN F.	CPL	INF
ARTHUR, ROY B.	PVT	INF
ASCHKENASY, ART A.	PVT	INF
BACHANT, HERBERT R.	PFC	INF
BACHMAN, WILLIAM J.	PFC	INF
BAILEY, FRED JR	PVT	INF
BAKER, CLYDE E.	S/SGT	INF
BAKER, JOY V.	PVT	INF
BAKER, LEONARD W.	PVT	INF
BATES, MARTIN E.	PFC	INF
BAZZLE, BENNIE L.	PVT	INF
BEARD, LOWELL B.	PFC	INF
BEASON, SAMUEL V.	PVT	INF
BECK, LOUIS A.	PVT	INF
BELOSTOCK, NATHAN A.	T/SGT	INF
BERG, ALFRED H.	PvT	INF
BERG, ARNOLD A.	PVT	INF
BERRETTA, ROSARIO E.	PVT	INF
BERTRAM, GEORGE F.	T/SGT	INF
BIDEWELL, LESTER E.	PVT	INF
BOWEN, GEORGE E.	PFC	INF
BOYD, CLARENCE W.	PFC	INF
BROWN, KENNETH	PVT	INF
BROWN, ROBERT L.	S/SGT	INF
BUCKNER, EDWARD G.	PVT	INF
BURROWS, CHARLES B.	TEC 5	MD
BUSHEY, OLIVER A.	PVT	INF
BUSTER, JAMES W.	TEC 5	INF
BUTLER, RAYMOND E.	PVT	INF

Name	Rank	Branch
CARDINELI, LEO NMI	TEC 5	INF
CARLSON, EDWIN H.	TEC 4	INF
CAROLLO, JERRY F.	PFC	INF
CHENOWETH, FRANK E.	PFC	INF
CHUBB, FLOYD E.	SGT	INF
CHUDNOFF, HERBERT	PVT	INF
CHURCH, BURLEY G.	CPL	INF
CICOTTI, JOHN P.	PFC	INF
COLLINS, LOREN D.	T/SGT	INF
COOK, LE ROY W.	T/SGT	INF
COOK, ROY E.	PFC	MD
CORCORAN, FRED E.	PFC	INF
CORDERO, PAUL JR	PVT	INF
CORRIGAN, RAYMOND A.	S/SGT	INF
CORTELLONI, RAY O.	PVT	INF
COUTCHER, RALPH E.	PVT	INF
COX, EDWIN D.	PFC	INF
CRISTIANO, VINCENT J.	PVT	INF
CRUSE, HAROLD R.	PFC	INF
CUBBAGE, MAURICE	PFC	INF
CUMBIE, FRED L.	CPL	INF
DADDI, JOSEPH	PFC	INF
DANIELS, FLOYD W.	PFC	INF
DAVENPORT, CHARLES C.	PFC	INF
DAVIS, LOUIS A.	PVT	INF
DAY, JAMES R.	PVT	INF
DE GENNERO MORRIS L.	PVT	INF
DEMPLER WALTER J.	1 LT	INF
DESMOND, PAUL T.	PVT	INF
DEVINE, WILLIAM C.	PVT	MD
DI CERBO LORENZO V.	PFC	INF
DE SYLVESTRO, JOHN M.	PFC	INF
DIANETTI, LEO	PVT	INF

DOSTATNI, JOSEPH J.	PFC	INF
DRIGGERS, WALTON C.	PVT	INF
DU FRAME, FRANKLIN J.	PVT	INF
DUKE, MILLS E.	PFC	INF
DWYER, LEO M.	S/SGT	INF
DZIEDZICKIE, CASMIR	T/SGT	INF
EDGELL, ROBERT C.	PFC	INF
ENGLISH, SAMUEL K.	T/SGT	INF
FAIRCHILD, ARDREY H.	PVT	INF
FAIREY, GEORGE H.	2 LT	INF
FARTHING, RAY J.	PFC	INF
FERGUSON, EVERETT W.	PVT	INF
FIELDING, EDWARD W.	T/SGT	INF
FIELDS, RAY E.	PFC	INF
FINCH, ROBERT B.	CAP	INF
FISCHER, ELMER H.	PVT	INF
FISH, EDWARD R.	PFC	INF
FISK, CALVIN R. JR	PVT	INF
FOSTER, HAROLD A.	PVT	MD
FRAPPIER, MAURICE A.	S/SGT	INF
FREY, FREDERICK H.	PVT	INF
FROMHARTZ, JOHN A.	TEC 5	INF
FULLER, JOHNNY A SR	TEC 5	INF
GALLAGER, R J JR	PFC	INF
GALLO, VINCENT F.	PFC	INF
GARWACKI, WILLIAM L.	SGT	INF
GAY, RALPH L.	S/SGT	INF
GETTY, VINCENT JR	S/SGT	INF
GIAMBATTISTA, JOHN R.	S/SGT	INF
GILLIAM, CLIFFORD L.	CPL	INF
GNIOT, CHARLES C. JR 1	LT	INF
GOLEC, PETER P.	PFC	INF
GOOD, REGINALD E.	CPL	INF

GOODELL, MELVIN E.	PFC	INF
GORDON, GEORGE J.	PFC	INF
GORNY, HENRY	SGT	INF
GOSSE, HERMSAN W.	S/SGT	INF
GREEN, EARL V. JR	2 LT	INF
GRENIER, HENRY L.	SGT	INF
GROOM, THOMAS E.	PFC	INF
GROVE, CHARLES E. JR	PFC	INF
GURSKI, CASIMER A.	PVT	INF
GUTSCHMIDT, ROBERT W. 1	LT	INF
HABEL, JOHN M. JR	PVT	INF
HARRINGTON, CLAYTON L	PFC	INF
HEINS, CHARLES L. JR	PFC	INF
HELMS, PAUL B.	PVT	INF
HENDRICKSON, MARCEL	S/SGT	INF
HICKS, GEORGE C.	SGT	ING
HILDENBRAND, T W	PFC	INF
HOFFERER, CARL J.	PFC	INF
HOKETT, JAMES S.	PFC	INF
HOLLAND, HARVEY C.	PFC	INF
HONNEFFER, HILDRETH C	PFC	INF
HUGHES, JAMES T.	PVT	INF
HUMPICK, FREDDIE G.	S/SGT	INF
HUNTSMAN, DENNIS D.	TEC 5	INF
JACKSON, CURTIS	SGT	INF
JOLLAY, PERRY D.	PVT	INF
JONES, ROY F.	PVT	INF
JUARAZ, ROBERT E.	PFC	INF
KALIL, LOUIS J.	TEC 5	INF
KANDEFER, FRANK J.	TEC 5	INF
KATZ, HOWARD C.	1 LT	INF
KAUFMAN, THEODORE NMI	SGT	INF
KEANE, FRANCIS X.	S/SGT	INF

KERLEY, FENIA P.	PVT	INF
KESSINGER, CLAYTON NM	PVT	INF
KING, EDWARD L. II	PVT	INF
KNAPP, ALBERT H.	PVT	INF
KNIGHT, HARRY F.	PFC	INF
KNIPP, KENNETH R.	PVT	INF
KOCHANSKI, PETER J.	T/SGT	INF
KOVACH, ANDY	PVT	INF
KREIDER, MILTON R.	PFC	INF
LANGE, ROBERT F.	CAP	INF
LASK, PETER J.	1 LT	INF
LAWLER, EDWARD J.	PVT	INF
LAZAR, HARRY	SGT	INF
LEAVITT, HAROLD L.	PVT	INF
LEECH, JAMES W.	CAP	INF
LHUILLIER, JOHN	CPL	INF
LIGHTFOOT, DAVID	PVT	INF
LINDSEY, CHARLES D.	PFC	INF
LINK, EDWARD F.	PVT	INF
LITTERAL, NEWT	S/SGT	INF
LONG, CLAYTON O.	PFC	INF
LONG, LELAND J.	PFC	INF
LONGORIO, JOHN S.	PVT	INF
LOVENBORG, STEN A.	PFC	INF
LOWRY, CLYDE D. JR	PVT	INF
LUBAS, FRANK A.	PFC	INF
LYON, GENE W.	PVT	INF
MAC MILLAN, KENNETH A.	PVT	INF
MACHOS, WALTER S.	PFC	INF
MAKAREWICZ, BENEDICT	TEC4	INF
MAKER, ROBERT B.	PFC	INF
MALLOY, EDWARD V.	S/SGT	INF
MALNOFSKI, FREDERICK	PVT	INF

MANEES, FRED M.	PFC	INF
MARCINKIEWICZ, WALLAC	S/SGT	INF
MARKLEY, WARREN R.	S/SGT	INF
MASON, FRANCIS L.	T/SGT	INF
MATTHEWS, HAROLD O.	PVT	INF
MATYASIK, JOSEPH A.	PVT	INF
MC CONNELL, DELBERT J	PFC	INF
MC CULLOUGH, JAMES	T/SGT	INF
MC ELWRATH, BROOKS	1LT	INF
MC FEELEY, RICHRD M	S/SGT	INF
MC GILL, ROBERT H. JR	PFC	INF
MC GOLTHIN, THERMAN	PFC	INF
MC HALE, PAUL J.	2LT	INF
MC KAGEN, FRANCIS A.	PFC	INF
MC KNNIGHT, EUGENE C.	PFC	INF
MC MASTER, GERGE W.	PFC	INF
MC MICHAEL, WILLIAM J.	PVT	INF
MC SHANE, JAMES A.	PFC	INF
MENARD, GUSTAVE E.	PFC	INF
MENDREY, STEPHEN R.	TEC 5	INF
MILLER, WILLIAM	PVT	INF
MINDRUP, JAMES G.	PFC	INF
MITCHELL, WILLIAM F.	2LT	INF
MOORE, DONALD L.	PVT	INF
MULLENAX, RAYMOND R.	PFC	INF
MURRAY, THOMAS A.	S/SGT	INF
MYERS, ROBERT F.	PVT	INF
NAPPA, VITO	PFC	INF
NELSON, GEORGE R.	T/SGT	INF
NOTTINGHAM, BENJAMIN	PVT	INF
OAKLEY, HUBERT L.	PFC	INF
ODER, RUBEN E.	PFC	INF
OTT, ALSON J.	PVT	INF

OTT, FRANCIS J.	S/SGT	INF
PADDOCK, THOMAS J.	PFC	INF
PATTON, WILLIAM P.	2LT	INF
PFOHL, JOSEPH W.	PFC	INF
PHILLIPS, WILLIAM C.	T/SGT	INF
PICCONE, JOSEPH J.	PVT	INF
PIERCE, CHARLIE M.	S/SGT	INF
PIERCE, LE ROY	S/SGT	INF
PLOG, CHARLES T.	PFC	INF
PLUFF, ANDREW C.	1LT	INF
PORTER, RAYMOND E.	PFC	INF
PURDY, RALPH F.	SGT	INF
QUENZER, EDWARD L.	TEC 5	INF
RALSTON, JAMES E.	PFC	INF
REASOR, JOHN L.	PFC	INF
REMICK, TIMOTHY D.	CPL	INF
REYNOLDS, AMOS	PFC	INF
RICHARDS, DAILE J.	PVT	INF
ROBINSON, RODNEY H.	PVT	INF
ROGERS, JAMES E.	PFC	INF
ROSOL, MICHAEL J.	PFC	INF
ROSS, ROY V.	PFC	INF
ROWE, WILLIAM T.	SGT	INF
ROY, OSCAR L.	PFC	INF
RUCINSKI, STANLEY J.	PFC	INF
RUGGIERO, EARNIE M.	TEC 5	INF
RYBAK, CASIMER F.	PFC	INF
SALES, JOHNATHAN E. JR	PVT	INF
SARGENT, CHARLES A.	T/SGT	INF
SCHERER, PAUL W.	PVT	INF
SCHWALB, NATHAN	PFC	INF
SEDILLO, ANTONIO B.	PVT	INF
SEELEY, CLAYTON L.	PVT	INF

SHARP, JOHN F, JR	TEC 5	INF
SHIRLEY, THOMAS O.	PFC	INF
SICIGNANO, RALPH J.	PFC	INF
SIFUENTES, NICASIO C.	PVT	INF
SILVERMAN, ISADORE M.	CAP	MC
SIMMONS, EARL T.	SGT	INF
SIMON, GARY C.	PFC	INF
SMITH, BRAYTON L.	PVT	INF
SMITH, JAMES T.	PVT	INF
SMITH, JOHN W.	TEC 5	INF
SMITH, OLIVER F.	PFC	INF
SMITH, RICHARD E.	PFC	INF
SMITH, TERRANCE C.	PVT	INF
SPAGNUOLO, VICTOR	PFC	INF
SPENCER, CARLTON M.	PFC	INF
SPOOR, JOHN R.	S/SGT	INF
SPRAY, DALL;AS C. JR	S/SGT	INF
STANLEY, EDWARD	TEC 5	INF
STANLEY, JACK W.	PFC	INF
STANLEY, JAMES W.	PFC	INF
STILLWAGNER, EDWARD E.	TEC 5	INF
STRAHOCKI, MICHAEL	PVT	INF
SWORD, CHARLES A.	PFC	INF
TABER, HENRY H.	PFC	INF
LAYLOR, ROY W.	PVT	INF
THOMAS, GREGORY	PVT	INF
THOMPSON, JOHN W.	PFC	INF
THRIFT, HASKELL	PVT	INF
TOWNE, CLARENCE A.	PFC	INF
TROUTMAN, MORRAW H.	PFC	INF
TSCHOPP, JAMES A.	PFC	INF
TURNER, CLIFFORD C.	T/SGT	INF
UPHAUS, JOHN W.	S/SGT	INF

URQUHART, ALBERT W.	PFC	INF
VECCHIO, JOSEPH	TEC 3	MD
VERVALIN, DONALD E.	TEC 5	INF
VICTOR, ROBERT J.	1 LT	INF
VINCENT, LATNEY	S/SGT	INF
VRABEL, STEPHEN C.	2 LT	INF
WALKER, PAUL S.	PFC	INF
WALSH, GEORGE J.	PFC	INF
WHITE, LAWRENCE L. JR	PFC	INF
WILLIAMS, CLAUDE M.	PFC	INF
WILLIAMS, JULIAN G.	PFC	INF
WILLIAMS, JOHN F.	SGT	INF
WILLIAMS, ROLLY J.	PVT	INF
WILSON, WILLIAM D.	1 LT	INF
WINDHAM, GERGE S.	PVT	INF
WINSTEAD, DANIEL E.	PVT	INF
WISNIEWSKI, CHESTER M.	PFC	INF
WOMBLE, SAM K.	T/SGT	INF
WOODS, JACOB	PFC	INF
WYLAND, JAMES E.	PVT	MD
YOUNG, ALTON E.	T/SGT	INF
YOUNG, THOMAS S.	PVT	INF
YUREHKO, ALEXANDER	PFC	INF
ZIELINSKI, GEORGE J.	PFC	INF
ZIMMERMAN, MEARL D.	PFC	INF
ZYDONIK, PAUL S.	PFC	INF

51ST ARMD INF BN

AGARD, ROBERT V.	SGT	INF
ALLEN, MALCOLM C.	SGT	INF
ALSTON, OLIE L.	2LT	INF
ANDERSON, CARL J.	PFC	INF

ANDERSON, PAUL E.	PFC	INF
AUSTIN, HENRY J.	SGT	INF
AYE, WILLIAM J.	PVT	INF
BAGGATT, EDGAR W. JR	TEC 5	INF
BAKER, DONALD J.	PVT	MD
BAKER, RAYMOND S.	CPL	INF
BARBIERI, DOMENICO	SGT	INF
BARENBERG, CLETUS W.	TEC 5	INF
BASS. WILLIAM O.	TEC 4	INF
BECK, JAMES Q.	PFC	INF
BENNETT, EARNEST R.	PFC	INF
BERRY, EDWARD J.	PFC	INF
BIERMANOSKI, S.F.	PVT	INF
BLANCHETTE, P.H. JR	CPL	INF
BLASO, ALEXANDER NMI	PVT	INF
BLOCK, WILLIAM A.	PFC	INF
BOCK, EDWIN	PVT	INF
BODNER, WILLIAM NMI	PVT	INF
BOYCE. SYDNEY F.	PFC	INF
BRANDENBERG, WILLIAM	S/SGT	INF
BRANSTETTER, FLOYD E.	PFC	INF
BRASTAD, MELVIN G.	PFC	INF
BRIDGES, JOSEPH C.	PFC	CE
BROWN, RAY E.	PFC	INF
BURGESS, JAMES M.	1LT	INF
BURL, GERALD B.	CPL	INF
BURTON, JAMES E.	PFC	INF
BUTLER, MAURICE A.	PVT	INF
CARVONA, DOMINIC P.	CAP	MC
CARLILE, FRANK U.	PFC	INF
CARRINGTON, RUFUS W.	PFC	INF
CERNY, CARL W.	S/SGT	INF
CHAMBERS, GEORGE B.	PVT	INF

CHAPPO, LOUIS	PFC	INF
CHILDS, RODGER F.	PVT	INF
CIEZAK, HENRY J.	CPL	INF
CISNEROS, FORTUNATO	PVT	INF
CLARK, ELBERT A.	PVT	INF
CLUTHE, ALBERT G.	PFC	INF
COLE, VERNON W.	2LT	INF
COLEMAN, JOHN H.	PVT	INF
COLLETT, ANDREW C.	1LT	INF
COMBS, EARNEST	PVT	INF
CONNER, HARRY W.	PVT	INF
CORMIER, ALFRED J.	PFC	INF
COSTANZO, VICTOR J.	PFC	INF
COTTRELL, AMOS K.	PVT	INF
CRANE, WILLIAM M.	CAP	INF
CREECH, WAYNE L.	CPL	INF
CUSSINS, LESTER R.	CPL	INF
DABBS, THOMAS L. JR	PFC	INF
DAHLWEINER, SAMUEL L.	PVT	INF
DE RUNGS, JACOB A.	2LT	INF
DECKER, ROBERT L.	PVT	INF
DECOSSE, RENE M.	CPL	INF
DELGADO, MANUEL	SGT	INF
DENTON, VIRGIL L.	PVT	INF
DEVEREAUX, ROBERT J.	PFC	INF
DEVINS, JOSEPH H.	PVT	INF
DI RICO, VICTOR J.	PFC	INF
DICKEY, WILIAM M.	CPL	INF
DISHMAN, ARTHUR E.	PFC	INF
DOLAN, DELMAR H.	PVT	INF
DOW, NORMAN E.	PFC	INF
DUFFORD, DONALD L.	PVT	INF
DUSENBERRY, HAROLD W.	PVT	MD

EGAN, PETER J.	PVT	INF
ELDER, JOHN L.	PFC	INF
ELSBERND, ALVIN J.	S/SGT	INF
EMERICK, MILTON R.	PFC	INF
ESPINOZA, BERNARD R.	PFC	INF
ESQUIVEL, THEODORE L.	TEC 5	INF
ESTRADA, MANUEL	PVT	INF
FAUBERT, JOSEPH J.	PVT	INF
FAVA, JAMES F.	TEC 4	INF
FAVORS, MARTIN J.	PFC	MD
FEHRENBACHER, F. J.	PVT	INF
FELTY, FRED E.	PVT	INF
FISHBURN, LEO T.	PFC	INF
FITTS, SAM T.	SGT	INF
FLANAGAN, DENVER O.	PFC	INF
FRANCIS, RUSSELL H.	2 LT	INF
FRENCH, ROBERT L.	1 LT	INF
GALLIPEAU, EUGENE H.	PFC	INF
GARBACK, EDWARD S.	PFC	INF
GARCIA, JULIO M.	SGT	INF
GARUCKIS, JOSEPH C.	S/SGT	INF
GILLAND, FRED	S/SGT	INF
GOLDBERG, IRVING	PVT	INF
GONZALES, JOSE R. JR	PVT	INF
GREENBERGER, MARVIN H.	PVT	INF
GREENWAY, RICHARD E.	PVT	INF
GRIFFIN, ARTHUR C. JR	CAP	INF
HALL, FLOYD G.	PFC	INF
HALL, FRANCIS J.	PFC	INF
HALL, VICTOR J.	TEC 5	INF
HALLER, WILLIAM E.	PFC	INF
HARRIS, ROBERT L.	S/SGT	INF
HAVARD, WILLIAM A.	PVT	INF

HAWTHORNE, WILLIAM M.	PVT	INF
HEFFERNAN, JOHN R.	PVT	INF
HEILMAN, HENRY	PFC	INF
HERMAN, RICHARD A.	PVT	INF
HERRING, JOHN W.	S/SGT	INF
HOBGOOD, CHARLES P. JR	S/SGT	INF
HOKE, JACK W.	1 LT	INF
HOLLOWAY, JAMES F.	PFC	INF
HOLZINGER, RUDOLPH E.	PFC	INF
HOPKINS, GEORGE W.	PVT	INF
HOPKINS, WILLIAM J.	S/SGT	INF
HOROWITZ, ISADORE I.	PFC	INF
HOVANEC, MICHAEL J.	T/SGT	INF
HOY, JAMES W.	PVT	INF
HRONICH, VINCENT T.	PFC	INF
HUGHES, MURWIN R.	PVT	INF
HYNES, JOSEPH W.	PFC	INF
IRVIN, LLOYD T.	CPL	INF
JAMNETSKI, FERDINAND	SGT	INF
JAYNES, ROSCOE M.	PFC	INF
JENNINGS, THOMAS S.	PFC	INF
JENSEN, CHARLES A.	PFC	INF
JOHNSON, FRANK L.	PVT	INF
KAMANDULIS, JOHN J.	PFC	INF
KAYSER, JOHN D.	2 LT	INF
KELLER, RAYMOND E.	PFC	INF
KELLY, DON P.	PFC	INF
KETTER, BILLY R.	PVT	INF
KEYSER, IGNATIUS B.	2 LT	INF
KINDER, VICTOR J.	PFC	INF
KING, LOUIS N.	PVT	INF
KIRKLEY, LOUIS L.	PFC	INF
KLEIN, GEORGR A.	PVT	INF

KLEPCHICK, ANTHONY A.	T/SGT	INF
KNOPP, WILLIAM R.	PFC	INF
KOZLOWSKI, CAZIMIR W.	TEC 5	INF
KRAJNA, HENRY F.	TEC 5	INF
LABBE, ROLAND J.	PFC	INF
LADO, ADELBERT P.	S/SGT	INF
LAHEY, ROBERT H.	2 LT	INF
LANDESS, JACK O.	PVT	INF
LANDINO, JAMES G.	TEC 5	INF
LARDNER, THOMAS E.	PVT	INF
LARSON, REYNOLD T.	PFC	INF
LATOCHE, FRANCIS J.	PFC	INF
LA BRON, RAYMOND	PVT	INF
LESKOVAR, RICHARD F.	1 LT	INF
LEVONCHUCK, WILLIAM N.	S/SGT	INF
LIFER, CHARLES E.	PFC	INF
LIPSCOMB, GEORGE T.	PFC	INF
LOWERY, HAROLD E.	S/SGT	INF
LUZIER, JUNIOR R.	PVT	INF
MADSEN, PAUL V.	PVT	MD
MAIER, WALTER C.	PFC	INF
MAJAROV, PETER	S/SGT	INF
MARKHAM, THOMAS L.	PVT	INF
MARSHALL, EDWARD F.	PFC	INF
MARSHALL, EDWARD A.	2 LT	INF
MARSHALL, THOMAS L.	S/SGT	INF
MARTIN, ALBERT B.	PVT	INF
NASH, EDGAR P.	PFC	INF
MAY PAUL E.	SGT	INF
MAYBACH, ALFRED A.	LT COL	INF
MAYER, FREDERICK J.	PFC	INF
MAYHLE, CECIl W.	PFC	INF
MC ABEE, LEE J.	PFC	INF

MC INTIRE, ROGER R.	2 LT	INF
MC NEIL, GUY R.	PVT	INF
MC SWEENEY, ARTHUR J.	S/SGT	INF
MEADOWS, GEORGE E.	PVT	INF
MEHAFFEY, ROLAND NMI	PVT	INF
MEHRTENS, JOHN W.	2 LT	INF
MENDEZ, HENRY	PFC	INF
MENGE, HAROLD	S/SGT	INF
METTS, WILLIAM J.	PVT	INF
MILLER, DONALD H.	2 LT	INF
MILLER, RICHARD S.	PFC	INF
MILLHORN, ARTHUR L.	PVT	INF
MILLS, DEMPSEY A.	SGT	INF
MILLS, WILLIAM M.	S/SGT	INF
MINOTILLO, PASQUALE	SGT	INF
MIZUTOWICZ, WALTER M.	PVT	INF
MOLONY, WILLIAM J.	PVT	INF
MONAGHAN, ROBERT N.	PVT	INF
MOORE, DAVID H.	PFC	INF
MOORE, LEONARD D.	PFC	INF
MORTSON, ROBERT C.	S/SGT	INF
MOSES, COLLINS	S/SGT	INF
MARWINSKI, DONALD A.	PVT	INF
MURRAY, HENRY M.	PVT	INF
MUZIO, CLEMENT	PVT	INF
NATHANSON, BERNARD	PFC	INF
NEVILLE, ROBERT P.	TEC 5	INF
NEWMAN, EDWARD H.	PVT	MD
NICGORSKI, PAUL W.	TEC 5	INF
NICOLETTI, EMIL	PVT	INF
NOE, HENRY NMI	PVT	INF
OAKLEY, HAROLD R.	PFC	INF
OHEARN, JAMES R.	PFC	INF

OLSON, ALVIN	PFC	INF
OLSON, WILLIAM W.	PFC	INF
OMDAHL, OLIVER G.	PVT	INF
OPOTOSKY, WALTER	T/SGT	INF
ORR, PERCY S.	PVT	INF
OSTLER, GRANDON H.	PVT	INF
PACHECO, RAUL A.	PFC	INF
PACK, CHARLES H.	PFC	INF
PACKARD, NORMAN E.	PFC	INF
PADILLA, RICHARD M.	PVT	INF
PARIS, WILLIAM T.	S/SGT	INF
PARKER, WILLIAM A.	PVT	INF
PEARSON, VICTOR L.	PFC	INF
PEC, JOSEPH G.	PVT	INF
PECK, RAYMOND	PVT	INF
PEEPLES, GEORGE W.	PVT	INF
PENLAND, CREED	PVT	INF
PERDUE, OMER J.	SGT	INF
PESSNELL, CECIL W.	PVT	INF
PETERSON, HOMER	PVT	INF
PHILLIPS, KIRBY A.	PFC	INF
PIERCE, ELLSWORTH K.	PFC	INF
POMERANTZ, MORRIS J.	PVT	INF
PRALLE, HELMUTH T.	S/SGT	INF
PRINCE, WALTER W.	PVT	INF
PRITCHETT, THOMAS W.	PFC	INF
PRUETT, JOHN W.	PFC	INF
PRUSINOWSKI, STANLEY	PFC	INF
PUCKETT, GUY	T/SGT	INF
RADOTICH, TOM	PFC	INF
RANDALL, RICHARD E.	PFC	INF
REGISTER, EARNEST A.	PVT	INF
REINHOLD, PAUL E.	PFC	INF

RINGER, JOSEPH E.	PVT	INF
ROBILLARD, ALFRED J.	PFC	INF
ROBINSON, DUNCAN E.	PVT	INF
ROBINSON, ELLIOTT D.	PVT	INF
ROCCO, STERLING L.	TEC 4	INF
ROMERO, TIMOTOE	PVT	INF
ROSS, FREDERICK E.	PFC	INF
ROTTMAN, LE ROY L.	PFC	INF
RUMFELT, JOSEPH B.	PVT	INF
RUSSELL, FRED F.	PVT	INF
SACCO, JOSEPH JR	PFC	INF
SALAZAR, ALCARIO C.	PFC	INF
SAN CLEMENTE, MARION	PVT	INF
SANDERS, ELLUS M.	PVT	INF
SANTOS, ANIBAL D.	PVT	INF
SAVAGE, CLAUDE J.	PVT	INF
SAVAGE, HARRY B.	S/SGT	MD
SAWICKI, JOSEPH A.	TEC 5	MD
SCALLEY, ROBERT B. JR	PVT	INF
SCHARZ, PHILLIP E.	T/SGT	INF
SCHNATZ, ROBERT R.	S/SGT	INF
SCHOENBAUM, RAYMOND D.	S/SGT	INF
SCHOFIELD, LLOYD L.	PFC	INF
SCHUMAN, HARRY N.	PFC	INF
SCOGGINS, GEORGE R.	PVT	INF
SERRA, JAMES V.	PVT	INF
SEYMOUR, FRANK L.	PFC	INF
SHARP, RALPH A.	PFC	INF
SHEARER, VERNON F.	PVT	MD
SHELEY, JOHN J.	PVT	INF
SHIRILLA, JOHN	PVT	INF
SHOULTS, HERMAN B.	SGT	INF
SINGLETON, MASON M.	PVT	INF

SKELTON, HAROLD C.	S/SGT	INF
SKIRBA, MARTIN J.	PFC	INF
SMITH, HOWARD E.	PVT	INF
SMITH, RAYMOND	PVT	INF
SMITH, WILLIAM J.	T/SGT	INF
SOUTHALL, WILLIAM D.	CPL	INF
SPLAWN, HALL J. JR	PFC	INF
STEPHENS, ERWIN R.	PFC	INF
STOLL, SAMUEL L.	PVT	INF
STOVASH, GEORGE E.	PFC	INF
STOVER, HERBERT C.	SGT	INF
STROUP, ROBERT A.	PVT	MD
SUMMERS, JOHN B.	PVT	INF
SWINSCOE, THOMAS	PVT	INF
SZELAG, HENRY W.	PFC	INF
TANNENBAUM, SOL	S/SGT	INF
TASCIONE, RALPH H.	PVT	INF
TAYLOR, JONATHAN S.	PVT	INF
THARP, DON F.	PVT	INF
THOMAS, ALBERT M.	S/SGT	INF
THOMAS, CHARLES W.	T/SGT	INF
THOMPSON, ELZA R.	SGT	INF
TICHENER, WILLIAM T.	S/SGT	INF
TEITJEN, FREDERICK JR	S/SGT	INF
TODD, JIMMY	PFC	INF
TRAIL, JOHN H.	PFC	INF
TREVINO, MAXIMO G.	PVT	INF
TRICKETT, HAROLD C.	PVT	INF
TROISI, GAETANO	S/SGT	INF
TROUP, KENNETH T.	TEC 5	INF
TSIKNAS, WILLIAM G.	CPL	INF
TURNER, GEORGE T.	PVT	INF
TUTTLE, RAYMOND H.	S/SGT	INF

UNDERWOOD, ESKER O.	PVT	INF
VACCA, JOHN A.	PFC	INF
VANDERKERKOVE, ROLAND	PFC	INF
VENTRELLA, TONY	PVT	INF
VERRY, WALTER R.	PVT	INF
VERAEY, TONEY P.	PVT	INF
WAGNER, KENNETH L.	2 LT	INF
WAGNER, LEONARD W.	PFC	INF
WALES, ALEXANDER H.	PVT	INF
WALKER, BERNNIE	PVT	INF
WALKER, LEONARD F.	PFC	INF
WALTERS, FLOYD W.	PVT	MD
WARD, CHARLES T.	PVT	MD
WENGER, RUSSELL	PVT	INF
WESTPHAL, ARNOLD F.	TEC 5	INF
WHITE, JAMES W.	PFC	INF
WILLIAMS, HARRY R.	PFC	INF
WILSON, RALPH W.	PVT	INF
WINSLOW, HERBERT C.	PFC	INF
WINTZ, URBAN G.	PFC	INF
WISE, FRED J.	PFC	INF
YELTON, SAMUEL A.	CPL	INF
ZAHN, SYLVAN A.	2 LT	INF
ZANETTI, LAWREN CE S.	PVT	
INF		

53RD ARMD INF BN

ABRAHAM. JEROME	PFC	MD
ALLEN, ROGER	PFC	INF
ALLORE, RAYMOND F.	PFC	INF
ALSHUK, WALTER	PFC	INF
ANTONOWITZ, JOHN	PFC	INF

AUERNHAMMER, VICTOR N.	PVT	INF
BACH, FREDERICK W.	PFC	INF
BACHMANN, JOHN P.	S/SGT	INF
BAKER, FERRELL A.	PFC	INF
BANICKY, MICHAEL	PVT	INF
BARKER, BILL	TEC 5	MD
BARLOW, JAMES E.	SGT	INF
BELCHER, JAMES A.	PFC	INF
BARRY, ERASTUS L.	PFC	INF
BLYTHE, LLOYD H.	2 LT	INF
BOUCHER, VERNON A. JR	SGT	INF
BOWLING, LOREN	PVT	INF
BOYD, PETE W.	PVT	INF
BROGAN, CREED	PVT	INF
BROWN, CARL H.	PVT	INF
BROWN, RAYMOND C.	PFC	INF
BUDROW, JOHN P.	PVT	INF
BUSCHMAN, HAROLD L.	S/SGT	INF
CARD, CLARENCE L.	PFC	INF
CARSTENS, HAROLD L.G.	PFC	INF
CASSIDY, CHESTER J.	PVT	INF
CASTELEIN, PAUL	SGT	INF
CHLUDZINSKI, EDWARD V.	PFC	INF
CICHOCKI, JOHN	SGT	INF
CLARK, FREDERICK L.	PFC	INF
CLEMENTS, ZACHARIE J.	SGT	INF
CLIFFORD, WILLIAM J.	PVT	INF
COCHRAN, JOSEPH D.	PVT	INF
COLLINS, CARL W.	PFC	INF
COX, JOHN W.	PFC	INF
CROCKER, ROY L.	PVT	INF
CROSCHERE, GERALD A.	SGT	INF
CURCIA, JOHN N.	PVT	INF

CURTIS, ROBERT E.	PFC	INF
CZARNEY, EDD	S/SGT	INF
CZARNOTA, PETER L.	S/SGT	INF
DALTON, CHARLES E.	PFC	INF
DANIELS, WILLIAM J. JR	TEC 4	INF
DARLING, EUGENE R.	PFC	INF
DAUGHENBAUGH, DALE E.	PFC	INF
DAVINER, BERTRAM F.	PVT	INF
DAVIS, DAVID H.	PVT	INF
DAVIS, JOHN E.	PFC	INF
DAVIS, LOUIS S.	PVT	INF
DE YOUNG, EDWARD R.	PVT	INF
DEMPSEY, NORMAN P.	S/SGT	INF
DERR, CARL W.	PVT	MD
DI LELLA, ADOLPH J.	PFC	INF
DOHERTY, JOHN J.	PFC	MD
DONAHUE, KENNETH G.	PFC	INF
DORSHEIMER, WILLIAM G.	PVT	INF
DOUGLASS, CHARLES A.	PFC	INF
DUFFY, JAMES SR	2 LT	INF
EBERSOHL, LUTHER E.	PFC	INF
EHRHARDT, ALEX	TEC 5	INF
ELMORE, FATE JR	PFC	INF
ENGLE, LAWRENCE C.	PVT	INF
ESHLEMAN, VIRGIL L.	S/SGT	INF
EVANS, WILLIAM H.	PFC	INF
FEDUSKA, PETER	PFC	INF
FEE, MARVIN L.R.	PVT	MD
FICK, 'EARL W.	PVT	INF
FIDDLE, SIDNEY	PVT	INF
FINEGAN, JOHN R.	CAP	INF
FLATH, JOHNW.	TEC 5	INF
FLOURNOY, JOHN H.	PVT	INF

FORD, ROBERT L.	SGT	INF
FOWLER, VERNON J.	T/SGT	INF
FOX, CLARENCE E. JR	S/SGT	INF
FOX, EARNEST R.	PVT	INF
FRASER, RAYMOND H.	PVT	MD
FRATELLI, DOMINIC F.	PFC	INF
GALLUCCI, JOSEPH A.	PVT	INF
GARLAND, HERSCHEL	PVT	INF
GARRETT, NOLAN L.	PVT	INF
GASIOROWSKI, HILARY P.	S/SGT	INF
GAYNOR, VICTOR F.	PVT	INF
GIBBS, JACK D.	PFC	INF
GIVEN, WAITMAN C. JR.	CPL.	INF
GOODMAN, LEONARD	T/SGT	INF
GORDON, LAWRENCE B.	SGT	INF
GRABOWSKI, THEODORE V.	PVT	INF
GRUNDY, FRANKLIN F. JR	TEC 5	INF
GUERRETTE, ALTHEODE R.	PVT	INF
GUNDY, HOWARD J.	1 LT	INF
HALBEISEN, HALDON L.	TEC 5	INF
HALL, JIMMY N.	SGT	INF
HALL, SAMUEL A.	PFC	INF
HAMILTON, GROVER M.	S/SGT	INF
HAMILTON, ORA B.	CPL	INF
HANSTROM, GLENN E.	TEC 5	INF
HARVELL, EDWARD G.	PVT	INF
HASLBECK, ROBERT H.	PFC	INF
HECKEL, STEPHEN J.	PFC	INF
HEIBERGER, JOHN J.	SGT	INF
HENDERSHOT, EARNEST R.	PFC	INF
HERBERT, GEORGE B. JR	1 LT	INF
HESS, EVERETT L.	2 LT	INF
HOLBEN, DONALD S.	PVT	INF

HOLKA, PETER J.	PFC	INF
HOY, LESTER L.	PFC	INF
HUCKS, ELLIOTT W.	PVT	INF
HUDGINS, LONZO	PVT	INF
HUSBAND, CALVIN J.	PVT	INF
HYATT, HERMAN L.	S/SGT	INF
INGERSOL, HERBERT L.	T/SGT	INF
INGRAM, ROY W.	S/SGT	INF
JACKSON, GEORGE A.	PVT	MD
JACKSON, HOMAN K.	S/SGT	INF
JACOBS, EARNEST R.	TEC 5	INF
JAKUBOWSKI, KAISEY J.	PFC	INF
JANCZURA, JOSEPH	PVT	INF
JARZYK, MICHAEL	PFC	INF
JERRAID, LOYD E.	S/SGT	INF
JIMENEZ, LEONARDO	PFC	INF
JOHNSON, ROGER E.	PFC	INF
JOHNSON, WALLACE O.	PVT	INF
JONES, JOHNNIE F.	S/SGT	INF
JONES, THEODORE S.	PFC	INF
JUNGBECK, DUNCAN M.	PFC	INF
JURECK, FRANCIS	PVT	INF
KARLO, RUDOLPH M.	PVT	INF
KEANE, WILLIAM H.	2 LT	INF
KETCHEL, VICTOR C.	1 SGT	INF
KEITH, LOVIC G.	PVT	INF
KEITH, SHERIDAN J.	PVT	INF
KEMP, HOMER E.	S/SGT	INF
KENNEY, JOSEPH L.	TEC 5	INF
KING, COLIN C.	S/SGT	INF
KING, WILLIAM A.	PVT	MD
KLINKOSKY, JOSEPH	PFC	INF
KNICKERBOCKER, R. H.	PFC	INF

KOEHLER, REUBEN F.	PFC	INF
KOSEK, JOHN F.	PVT	INF
KOZLOWSKI, RAYMOND E.	PFC	INF
KUZUPAS, CHARLES	S/SGT	INF
LARSEN, LEROY A.	SGT	INF
LARSON, HAROLD W.	PFC	INF
LAUBE, EDWARD W. JR	PFC	INF
LAVITOLA, NICHOLAS	PFC	MD
LEE, ROBERT E.	PFC	INF
LEWIS, JESSE L.	T/SGT	INF
LO PRESTI, GEORGE J.	S/SGT	INF
LONGANO, JOHN	PFC	INF
LUKASZEWSKI, WALTER J.	S/SGT	INF
MACHEK, JERRY A.	PVT	INF
MACRI, VINCENT F.	S/SGT	INF
MANALE, BERNARD J. JR	PFC	INF
MARTHER, RICHARD D.	PVT	INF
MARTIN, FRANCIS W.	PFC	INF
MARTIN, ROBERT E.	PVT	INF
MARVEL, WILLIAM S.	PVT	INF
MATZKE, HOWARD R.	2 LT	INF
MAZUR, MICHAEL F.	SGT	INF
MC CORMACK, E J JR	2 LT	INF
MC CULLICK, HARRY W.	S/SGT	INF
MC DERMOTT, LAURENCE	PVT	INF
MC KELROY, WAYNE B.	PFC	INF
MC PHEE, WILLIAM A.	TEC 5	INF
MEDINA, MIGUEL	PFC	INF
MELIES, ROBERT W.	PFC	INF
MENCARELLI, ALDINO	TEC 5	INF
METZNER, CHARLES H.	PVT	INF
MIANNAY, EDWARD E.	TEC 5	INF
MICHAEL, WESLEY W.	S/SGT	INF

MICHAUD, ADRIEN J.	PFC	INF
MILLER, MARVIN D.	PVT	INF
MINTON, CARL	PVT	INF
MISEWICZ, LEON	SGT	INF
MITCHELL, ROY	T/SGT	INF
MOOMAW, STEVENSON	PFC	MD
MOREIRA, ARMENIO	PVT	INF
MULBERRY, J W	PFC	INF
MURGA, GEORGE	PFC	INF
MYERS, CARL E.	PVT	INF
NEGRA, WILLIAM H.	T/SGT	INF
NICHOLS, FRED W.	TEC 5	INF
NICHOLSON, HOWARD J.	PFC	INF
NOFFSINGER, TED	SGT	INF
NOTEIS, JOHN JR	PFC	INF
NOVAK, JERRY J.	SGT	INF
OFFSIANIK, GEORGE E.	PVT	INF
OHLER, WILLIAM H.	TEC 4	INF
OLNHAUSEN, RICHARD M.	S/SGT	INF
OWENS, ROBERT E.	PFC	INF
QWINGS, LESLEY J.	S/SGT	INF
PAULEY, NORMAN T.	PFC	INF
PEAK, FRANK L. JR	T/SGT	INF
PELL, THOMAS E.	CAP	INF
PETERSON, CLAIR E.	SGT	INF
PETERSON, JOHN M.	S/SGT	INF
PHILLIPS, JAMES W.	PVT	INF
PIHLSTROM, ALBERT K.	S/SGT	INF
RAMSEY, ROMIE	PVT	MD
RAND, EDWARD D.	PFC	INF
REED, LEONARD W.	SGT	INF
REED, ROBERT R.	TEC 5	INF
RIDDLE, ROBERT A.	PVT	INF

RILEY, JOHN W.	PFC	INF
ROBESON, CHARLES R.	PFC	INF
ROMERO, JESUS	PFC	INF
ROSS, ESTILL	PFC	INF
ROSS, ROBERT J.	PVT	INF
ROWLAND, DANIEL E.	TEC 5	INF
RUIZ, PORFIRIO S.	PFC	INF
SALAS, MYER	PFC	INF
SALERNO, NICHOLAS	PVT	INF
SANCHEZ, ANGEL	S/SGT	INF
SAP, LEE F.	S/SGT	INF
SCHISLER, LOUIS J. JR	S/SGT	INF
SHANLEY, EDWARD	1 LT	INF
SHEWAN, RICHARD W.	1 LT	INF
SMITH, REGINALD F.	SGT	INF
SMITH, WILLIAM G.	TEC 5	INF
SONSIADEK, BRUNO	PFC	INF
SPACK, GEORGE T.	PFC	INF
SPROUSE, JOSEPH W.	PVT	INF
ST. GERMAIN, BERNARD W.	PVT	INF
STABILE, FRANK J.	PVT	INF
STEFFE, ARNOLD W.	PVT	INF
STOTTS, JOHN F	PFC	INF
STOUT, DONOVAN M.	PVT	INF
STOVER, WILBUR E.	PFC	INF
SWAIN, HAROLD L.	SGT	INF
SWOPE, ROBERT B.	PFC	INF
SZKURKA, FRANCIS	TEC 4	MD
TARSITANO, DOMINIC T.	TEC 4	INF
TAUBENSEE, JAMES E.	PFC	INF
TAYLOR, ELMER R.	PFC	INF
TAYLOR, MONROE	PFC	INF
TENCH, ROBERT H.	PVT	INF

THOMAS, MICHAEL A.	PFC	INF
THOMPSON, FRED B.	S/SGT	INF
TIBBY, ARTHUR R.	PVT	INF
TOBIN, CHARLES F.	T/SGT	INF
TOLSON, GEORGE W.	PFC	INF
TOMMILLO, PETER A.	S/SGT	INF
TORZILLO, LOUIS A.	PVT	INF
TRAIL, BERNARD	PFC	INF
TRAUB, JOSEPH L.	SGT	INF
TROVATO, MARIO B.	PVT	MD
TURNER, WAYNE C.	TEC 5	INF
UNGER, LEE H.	PFC	INF
UNGLENK, WILLIAM J.	PFC	INF
URICHER, WILLIAM	S/SGT	INF
URSO, JULIO G.	PVT	INF
VAN ETTEN, HOWARD L.	TEC 5	INF
VAN WINKLE, VIRGIL	S/SGT	INF
VARGA, PAUL E	S/SGT	INF
VERDEJA, CELESTINO N.	PFC	INF
VICK, DAVID A.	SGT	INF
VILLAREAL, MIGUEL	PVT	INF
VINSON, CHARLES E. III	PVT	INF
VLARICH, JOHN G.	PFC	INF
VOLZ, ROBERT R.	CAP	INF
WADE, LAWRENCE W.	PVT	INF
WALD, RICHARD O.	PVT	INF
WALN, VINCENT O.	TEC 5	INF
WALTER, GEORGE W.	PFC	INF
WAMSLEY, BOB D.	SGT	INF
WARD, CASSIE W. JR	PVT	INF
WEAVER, RICHARD E.	SGT	INF
WEINBERG, ADOLPH E.	S/SGT	INF
WELTER, VERNON T.	PVT	INF

WELZ, HERBERT W.	PVT	INF
WEST, GLENN M.	PFC	INF
WHETEN, JAMES	SGT	INF
WHITE, FRED C.	PVT	INF
WHITE, JAMES L.	PFC	INF
WHITE, OSCAR JR	S/SGT	INF
WHITSON, WILLIAM H.	PVT	INF
WILLIAMA, TURNER H.	TEC 4	INF
WILSON, FREDERICK H.	PVT	INF
WILSON, ROBERT B.	PFC	INF
WILSON, WOODROW	PVT	INF
WOODS, KENNETH W.	PVT	INF
WORTHEY, ORVIS R.	PVT	INF
ZICKUR, FRANK D. JR	S/SGT	INF
ZIEMAN, ROBERT W.	PFC	INF
ZIMMERMAN, MARVIN C.	PVT	INF
ZOMP, JOHN	SGT	INF

22ND ARMD FA BN

BORCZYK, RAYMOND C.	CPL	FA
CAMPBELL, GROVER F.	TEC 5	FA
CARCHIDI, JOSEPH A.	PFC	FA
CARSON, JOSEPH D.	SGT	FA
CLARKE, DENNY T.	PVT	FA
COSTELLO, LOUIS M.	PVT	FA
DOMINO, JOSEPH	PFC	FA
DUNCHOCK, JACK	PFC	FA
EDWARDS, EVERETT	PVT	FA
HANSEN, GLEN L.	TEC 5	FA
HOOD, CARVEL C.	1 LT	FA
HOSKINS, DELBERT R.	PFC	FA
KRAUSS, GEORGE E.	TEC 4	FA
LACEY, PAUL J.	PVT	FA

LEMANOWICZ, HENRY S.	CPL	FA
MC CRACKEN, CHARLES E.	2 LT	FA
MC GUCKEN, CHARLES E.	SGT	FA
MOORE, DAVID F.	1 LT	FA
SCHOCKMAN, WILLIAM J.	TEC 5	FA
SMITH, LOUIS W.	1 LT	FA
SUPPA, RALPH J.	PVT	FA
THORNTON, DONALD W.	SGT	FA
TOWNSEND, STANLEY C.	TEC 5	FA
ZAISER, HOWARD O.	CAP	FA

66TH ARMD **FA BN**

AINSWORTH, CLAUDE W.	PVT	FA
ANDREJANSKI, PAUL J.	TEC 5	FA
BANDEL, GEORGE P.	S/SGT	FA
BASCA, MICHAEL M.	CPL	FA
BOLEY, JOHNNY L.	PFC	FA
BROWN, HERBERT L. JR	PVT	FA
BUSHEME, FRANK R.	TEC 4	FA
CARTY, RAYMOND S.	PVT	FA
CROSS, EDWARD	PVT	FA
DAVIDSON, ROBERT W.	PVT	FA
DOYLE, CLARENCE E.	TEC 5	FA
DROSS, JOSEPH A.	PFC	FA
DWYER, THOMAS J.	CPL	FA
GAJDOS, PAUL	SGT	FA
GIOBBI, ARTHUR A.	TEC 4	FA
HANCOCK, GEORTGE E.	PFC	FA
HECKEL. CHARLES D.	T/SGT	FA
KALBFLEISCH, JOSEPH G.	CAP	FA
LEE, JAMES	PVT	FA
LEIBY, JACOB D.	PVT	FA
MAY, LEWIS H.	1 LT	FA

MORRIS, WILLIAM T.	PFC	FA
MROZEK, ANDREW J.	PFC	FA
MUMMA, DONALD E.	1 LT	FA
MYERS, STEPHEN G.	SGT	FA
NOLAN, FRANCIS P.	CPL	FA
NYS, EARL J.	CPL	FA
REIM, CHARLES W. JR	TEC 5	FA
REJRAT, EDWARD A.	2 LT	FA
RUTHERFORD, G. E. JR	1 LT	FA
SACCHINI, SOCONDO J.	SGT	FA
SANDERS, JOHN W.	PFC	FA
SANDERS, STANLEY L.	1 LT	FA
SAQUET, RAYMOND L.	CPL	FA
SCANLON, WILBERT D.	PFC	FA
WATSON, ROBERT S.	CAP	FA
WILLIAMS, EUGENE V.	1 LT	FA
WULF, BERTRAND C.	1 LT	FA
YECKER, VINCENT L.	TEC 5	FA

94TH ARMD FA BN

ADAMSON, GEORGE H.	PFC	FA
BRITT, OSCAR W.	TEC 4	FA
CHAPPELL, ELSBURY P.	PVT	FA
CHARLES, DRAPER J.	PFC	FA
CLARK, RUSSELL J.	TEC 5	FA
COSSEY, KENNETH W.	CPL	FA
DAVIDOVITCH, SAMUEL	PVT	FA
DUGAN, NORMAN J.	PFC	FA
DUBOVY, ALEXANDER	TEC 5	FA
EPPELE, WILLIAM	TEC 4	FA
GREENWALT, VICTOR H.	PVT	FA
HUFF, GORDON	TEC 4	FA

KELLY, JOHN F.	1 LT	FA
KLENK, ROBERT J.	PVT	FA
KOSIOROWSKI, CHARLES	SGT	FA
LEWIS, LIGE	PVT	FA
MAZZA, ANTHONY A.	SGT	FA
NORMAN, RUDOLPH	PVT	FA
OAKMAN, OSCAR B.	PFC	FA
ORSBON, HERMAN L.	S/SGT	FA
RAMEY, DONALD C.	PVT	FA
RICH, CARL W.	SGT	FA
RUBINFELD, DAVID	CPL	FA
SMITH, BOW	PVT	FA
SHOOK, JOSEPH A.	TEC 5	FA
TALLEY, HARMON W.	PFC	FA
WALLRAVEN, WILLIAM H.	TEC 4	FA
WEISSMAN, GEORGE	PVT	FA

25TH CAV RECON

ANCHORDOQUY, MARTIN J.	2 LT	CAV
ARNDT, ROBERT C.	SGT	CAV
AULT. FRANCIS E.	PFC	CAV
BAIRD, WILLARD E.	PVT	CAV
BARTLETT, ALAN M.	PVT	CAV
BENNETT, JAMES A .	2 LT	CAV
BENOIT. HENRY	TEC 5	CAV
BROWN, GROVER L.	CPL	CAV
BROEN, JOHN A.	PVT	CAV
BUELTEL, ALPHONSE D.	TEC 5	CAV
BUGG, HERMAN L.	2 LT	CAV
BYRAM, WALTER T.	2 LT	CAV
CANELLI, ALBERT G.	PVT	CAV
CARDEN, HARRY E.	TEC 5	CAV

CARUSO, GENARO A.	TEC 5	CAV
CENTER, WALTER H. JR	PVT	CAV
CHALUPA, LAWRENCE F.	SGT	CAV
CHANDA, JOHN	TEC 4	CAV
CLAMPFFER, ROBERT R.	TEC 4	CAV
COGDILL, CATL W.	CPL	CAV
CONDE, JOSEPH A.	PVT	CAV
CRAVETZ, PAUL P.	TEC 4	CAV
CROSWELL, BENNY W.	1/SGT	CAV
DE BUHR, CLARENCE	2 LT	CAV
DELP, JAMES E.	2 LT	CAV
DOWDESWELL, ROY	TEC 5	CAV
DRURY, JAMES J.	PFC	CAV
DUGAN, LEO F.	TEC 5	CAV
EVE, NICHOLAS V.	1/SGT	CAV
EWING, VIRGIL	TEC 5	CAV
FOX, JAMES O.	TEC 5	MD
GALLO, ARTHUR B.	S/SGT	CAV
GATES, FLOYD E.	S/SGT	CAV
GRANT, GEORGE W.	SGT	CAV
GRAVES, JOHN A.	TEC 4	CAV
GRGURICH, EDWARD	PVT	CAV
HARRIS, STOCKDON	PVT	CAV
HOWARTH, ALEXANDER A.	CPL	CAV
HULLE, EDWARD V.	TEC 5	CAV
HUSCHKA, ADAM G.	PFC	CAV
ITULE, LOUIE J.	CPL	CAV
KIMPEL, HAROLD C.	2 LT	CAV
KING, ARLEY D.	PFC	CAV
KONDOKOR, FRANK J.	PFC	CAV
KRUSE, MELVIN L.	PVT	CAV
LANDAU, MILTON F.	PVT	CAV
LEONETTI, FRANK	PFC	CAV

LEVERING, CHARLES R.	PVT	CAV
LYONS, WALTER H.	S/SGT	CAV
MAKELA, TENHO K.	1 LT	CAV
MICK, GEORGE H.	TEC 5	CAV
MOSKOWITZ, ABE	PVT	CAV
NILES, RONALD J.	TEC 5	CAV
OCHSNER, LEON	SGT	CAV
OCONNOR, JOHN S.	TEC 5	CAV
PARSLEY, LLOYD E.	TEC 5	CAV
PATTON, CLARENCE	TEC 5	CAV
PAYSON, ERROL E.	PVT	CAV
PETERSON, RICHARD A.	TEC 5	CAV
PHILLIPS, WILLIAM F.	TEC 4	CAV
RAYBON, CARL E.	PVT	CAV
RODRIGUEZ, SAM	PFC	CAV
ROGERS, EDWARD L.	TEC 5	CAV
SANTOS, JAMES L.	PVT	CAV
SAWICKI, LOUIS S.	TEC 5	CAV
SILVERMAN, HARRY S.	PVT	CAV
SIMEONE, RAYMOND J.	PFC	CAV
SKLAR, FRED	CAP	CAV
SMITH, EARL C.	2 LT	CAV
STIBER, JOSEPH F.	PFC	CAV
STITES, CHARLES W.	TEC 5	CAV
SYNORACKI, THADDEUS, J	TEC 4	CAV
TAYLOR, JESS B. JR	PFC	CAV
THERIAULT, ADRIEN L.	PFC	CAV
VOELKER, HENRY C.	SGT	CAV
WARDEN, GLENN L.	PVT	CAV
WASHBURN, MARVIN W.	PVT	CAV
WELLING, PETER C.	1 LT	CAV
WHITESCARVER, IVAN	TEC 5	CAV
WOLKE, NORBERT J.	PVT	CAV

YOUNG, ALAN D.	TEC 5	CAV
YOUNG, GEORGE B.	SGT	CAV

24TH ARMD ENGR BN

BECKWITH, LESLIE W. JR	CPL	CE
BIONDO, EARNEST J.	TEC 3	MD
BURGESS, JAMES T.	PFC	CE
CHILDREY, LOUIS A.	TEC 5	CE
CLEMENT, JAMES T.	PFC	CE
CORRIVEAU, LEONIDE J.	TEC 5	CE
CRUSE, NOLAN B. JR	PVT	CE
DE ZWAAN, STANLEY	PVT	CE
DUUTTON, KENNETH F.	1 LT	CE
ERLENBUSCH, JACOB	TEC 5	CE
EURE, LUTHER A.	TEC 5	CE
FORD, JOSEPH T. JR	S/SGT	CE
FRISBEE, VERNON	PVT	CE
GELLESPIE, EDWIN A.	S/SGT	CE
GOSS, DAVID P.	TEC 5	CE
HAJDAMOWICZ, JOSEPH J.	PFC	CE
HANDIBOE, MICHAEL F.	CAP	CE
HUSSEY, GEORGE E.	TEC 5	CE
JUNGMAN, ROBERT E.	2 LT	CE
KANDLER, LEWIS C.	PFC	CE
KAPETANOPOLIS, COSMOS	PVT	CE
KLICK, BERNARD C.	TEC 5	CE
LANE, EUEL M.	CPL	CE
LEGENDRE, EMILE	PFC	CE
LEPARE, JOSEPH E.	TEC 5	CE
MATORIN, MAURICE J.	PVT	CE
PETERS, GURMAN E.	PVT	CE
PETT, ARTHUR N.	S/SGT	CE

PIERI, FRANCIS W.	CAP	CE
PLICHTA, JOSEPH A.	PFC	CE
PUTNAM, EDWIN O.	TEC 4	CE
RIZZARDI, JOE P.	PVT	CE
ROY, HAROLD D.	PFC	CE
SMITH, IVAN T.	PFC	CE
STOCKDALE, ROBERT A.	S/SGT	CE
TEBA, SAMMY B.	PFC	CE
TOEDTLI, WILLIAM	TEC 5	CE
URBAN, WILLIAM P.	SGT	CE
WATERHOUSE, HOWARD G.	TEC 5	CE
WELCH, JOSEPH D.	TEC 5	CE
WHITE, GEORGE R.	TEC 4	CE
WICKLAND, ROLAND H.	S/SGT	CE
WORKMAN, CHARLES W.	PFC	CE
ZELLERS, EUGENE H.	SGT	CE

8TH ARMD TANK BN

ANDERSON, RUDY J.	PVT	INF
ARMSTRONG, WALTER E.	PVT	INF
ARO, TAUNO H.	CPL	INF
AUG, JAMES L.	TEC 5	INF
AUSTIN, LOUIS M.	PVT	AMD
BAILEY, MELVYN E.	1/SGT	INF
BAKAYSA, JOSEPH E.	PVT	INF
BAKER, RAYMOND H.	PVT	AMD
BALCUNS, JOSEPH	S/SGT	AMD
BARLOW, JOSEPH B.	TEC 5	INF
BEALS, ARTHUR M.	PVT	AMD
BELLISSIMO, DOMINICK	CPL	INF
BLACKMER, WILLIAM K.	1 LT	INF
BOWLES, LAWRENCE R.	PVT	INF

BRANDON, HARRY E.	PVT	INF
BROWN, WILLIAM H.	PVT	INF
BURDEN, WILLIAM E.	TEC 4	INF
BURNS, FRANK J.	PFC	AMD
BURTON, EUGENE F.	TEC 4	INF
CARGE, GEORGE	S/SGT	INF
CARNEY, ALBERT J.	TEC 5	INF
CERONE, FRANK	TEC 4	AMD
CHILLS, GEORGE M.	PVT	INF
CISCHKE, HERMAN C.	PFC	INF
CLEMONS, WAYNE J.	PVT	INF
COX, CYRIL T.	SGT	INF
CUNNINGHAM, JOSEPH M.	SGT	INF
DERLEGA, EDWARD	TEC 4	INF
DIAMANTI, ALBERT C.	PVT	INF
DUFFY, PAUL P.	TEC 5	INF
FELTNER, CARTER	CPL	INF
FERGUSON, HUBERT	CPL	INF
FISHER, ROY B.	SGT	INF
FLOMENBAUM, SEYMOUR	PVT	INF
FOGLIO, JOSEPH A.	TEC 5	INF
FRANK, STUART L.	TEC 4	INF
FRETENBOROUGH, C. F.	PFC	AMD
GJERS, ELDEN E.	PFC	INF
GRAVES, CLYDE	PVT	INF
GUILBEAU, LAZAIRE P.	TEC 5	AMD
GURKA, EDWARD N.	S/SGT	INF
HAMMOND, ORSON S.	1 LT	INF
HARWOOD, HARRY S. JR	TEC 5	INF
HEATH, JOHN E.	PVT	INF
HEIDEN, JACK A.	CPL	INF
HENSLEY, ELVIN J.	T/SGT	INF
HIERZ, HENRY	CPL	INF

HILL, CARL D.	PFC	AMD
HORVATH, JOHN J.	SGT	INF
HOUSE, RICHARD C.	TEC 5	INF
IMM, MARVIN A.	SGT	AMD
JENSEN, OTTO	SGT	AMD
KAMENSKY, GEORGE J.	1 LT	INF
KANTZ, RICHARD O.	PVT	INF
KEATING, CHARLES G.	SGT	INF
KELLY, JAMES C.	CPL	INF
KIPPLINGER, ROBERT C.	TEC 4	INF
KIRSHENBAUM, ISADORE	S/SGT	INF
KITTS, JAMES E.	S/SGT	AMD
KLINGA, CONSTANT A.	SGT	AMD
LASATER, CLYDE M.	PVT	INF
LOEWEN, DAVID S.	PVT	INF
MARSHALL, CLAYTON C.	PVT	INF
MASSEY, JACK W.	SGT	AMD
MATZ, PAUL L.	PFC	INF
MEADOWS, JAMES L.	CPL	INF
MEENA, JAMES F.	1 LT	CAV
MICHAELS, NICHOLAS J.	PFC	AMD
MICHALOVIC, HENRY W.	CPL	INF
MILISITS, JOE J.	TEC 4	AMD
MILNE, BRITTON J.	S/SGT	AMD
MONACO, DOMINICK	TEC 5	INF
MOZDZEN, CHESTER L.	CPL	INF
NICHOLAS, JOHNNIE L.	PFC	AMD
OTOOLE, B.D. JR	1 LT	INF
PATTERSON, GEORGE I.	TEC 5	INF
PAUTLER, CORNELIUS W.	SGT	INF
PIRIE, JAMES M.	CAP	INF
PITTORINO, JOSEPH	S/SGT	INF
PORR, DALE B.	T/SGT	AMD

PUNCH, ROBERT E.	PFC	INF
RAVASIO, BERNARD A.	PVT	AMD
RICE, WILLIAM L.	1 LT	INF
ROMANOFSKY, WALTER	PFC	AMD
ROMERO, EPIMENIO	PFC	INF
ROSSSI, JOSEPH E.	TEC 4	INF
RUNNION, JOSEPH C.	TEC 4	AMD
SETZKE, RAYMOND O.	PVT	AMD
SILVA, GENE W.	PFC	INF
SOUTHWORTH, PAUL W.	TEC 4	AMD
SPAGNA, LOUIS D.	1/SGT	INF
SPRINGER, WILLIAM L.	TEC 4	INF
STAKLEY, JOHN F.	TEC 5	AMD
STENZEL, LLOYD C.	CPL	INF
STEPHENS, VIRGIL H.	SGT	INF
STOUT, RAYMOND D.	S/SGT	INF
STREET, HAROLD A.	PVT	INF
TAYLOR, FRED	TEC 5	INF
TOMCZYK, MATTHEW A.	PFC	AMD
TRIMBACK, ROBERT R.	TEC 5	INF
TURMAN, MILTON T.	PVT	INF
WALKER, GEORGE E.	PFC	INF
WEAR, HOWARD H.	CPL	INF
WESTGATE, RAYMOND C.	PFC	INF
WISNIEWSKI, JOHN E.	SGT	AMD
WOOD, STANLEY F.	PVT	INF

35TH ARMD TANK BN

BEARS, JAMES W.	PVT	INF
BERG, CLETUS J.	PVT	AMD
BERNAL, ALEXANDER J.	SGT	INF
BIGGERSTAFF, MAX E.	2 LT	CAV

BONDER, JOHN	SGT	INF
BROWN, HERBERT E.	PVT	INF
BROWN, STANLEY A.	SGT	INF
CAPPELLETTI, FRANK	PFC	INF
CARDONE, WILLIAM	PVT	INF
CAROTHERS, PAUL R.	PVT	INF
CASTRO, JOSE	TEC 5	AMD
CHAPMAN, WILLIAM E.	CPL	INF
CHERMAK, JEROME	CPL	INF
CLAYTON, HERBERT W.	S/SGT	INF
CLEMENS, SCOTTY E.	TEC 4	AMD
CLINE, JOHN F.	1 LT	INF
CONHEADY, JAMES I. JR	PFC	AMD
COOPER, MARVIN R.	PFC	INF
CUDDY, JOHN L.	TEC 5	INF
CUTRONE, JOHN	TEC 5	INF
DANIELS, HENRY JR	PFC	INF
DE PALO, JOSEPH	SGT	INF
EDGECOMBE, HOWARD W.	S/SGT	INF
EDMONDS, JAMES C.	TEC 4	INF
ERARDI, JOSEPH JR	PVT	INF
EVENGA, ALEXANDER	1 LT	INF
FARMER, EARNEST D.	PVT	AMD
FEIERBERG, MAX	SGT	AMD
GILBERT, FRANK	PVT	INF
GROSS, LESLIE V.	SGT	AMD
GURRELL, FORD J.	TEC 5	AMD
HAGGERTY, VERN R.	PFC	INF
HALL, EVERETT E.	SGT	INF
HERBST, RICHARD G.	SGT	INF
HILL, HARRY R.	2 LT	INF
HILLARD, CHARLES P.	PFC	AMD
HOCK, CHARLES W.	PFC	AMD

HOCKETT, JAMES A.	TEC 4	INF
HUSER, LAWRENCE T.	CPL	INF
KARAS, PERRY J.	PVT	AMD
KELLY, THOMAS W.	PVT	INF
KIMBRELL, JIM	PVT	INF
LA SAVAGE, WALTER J.	TEC 5	INF
LAUGHLIN, PAUL G.	PVT	INF
LOPEZ, CHARLES W.	PVT	AMD
LOUKS, RUSSELL L.	PFC	INF
MACCHIAVELLO, WILLIAM	TEC 4	INF
MARINELLI, WILLIAM A.	CPL	AMD
MARTIN, JOHN D.	CPL	INF
MC DONALD, RALPH L.	CPL	INF
MC KENNEY, RICHARD D.	PFC	INF
MC LAIN, ROBERT A.	PFC	INF
MC NEES, WILLIAM	PFC	INF
MERCIE, JOSEPH E.	CPL	INF
MERCON, LOUIS	CPL	INF
MESSINA, SAMUEL J.	CPL	INF
MILAKOVICH, PETER A.	SGT	INF
MILLER, ISAAC	SGT	AMD
MORAN, JOHN J.	CPL	INF
NAGY, CHARLES A.	CPL	INF
NOLL, MARCELLE A.	PVT	INF
PAUCIELLO, EUGENE J.	S/SGT	AMD
PHILLIPS, ROBERT E.	PVT	INF
PRINGLE, PAUL E.	S/SGT	AMD
QUINN, PETER L.	TEC 4	INF
RAPAVI, PAUL	TEC 4	INF
RICH, LEONARD C.	TEC 5	INF
ROBBINS, CHARLES A.	SGT	INF
ROUNSAVALL, ELMO F.	1 LT	CAV
SCATTONE, VICTOR P.	TEC 4	INF

SCHNEBELEN, STANLEY D.	CPL	INF
SCHROEDER, NORBERT F.	CPL	AMD
SHIRLEY, ARCHIE W.	CPL	INF
SCHLEY, ROY E.	PFC	INF
SMARR, JOHN R.	PFC	INF
STEVENS, CLIFFORD E.	CPL	INF
THOMAS, RICHARDSON L.	PFC	INF
TOBIN, HARLAN W.	PVT	INF
TOMME, NEAL J.	PFC	INF
TRAIL, BERNARD J.	CPL	INF
VINGO, LOUIS W.	SGT	INF
WATSON, ALDEN C.	S/SGT	INF
WELLS, JAMES W.	2 LT	INF
WERTZ, ELDORE W.	CPL	INF
WHETSEL, ARTHUR L.	CPL	AMD
WILK, LESTER C.	SGT	AMD
WISHNIESKI, JOSEPH M.	SGT	INF
WOLF, LESTER L.	TEC 5	INF
WOOD, OTIS A. JR	CPL	AMD
WRIGHT, WALTER	CPL	AMD
ZENKEWICH, ANTHONY J.	SGT	INF

37TH ARMD TANK BN

ABRAHAM, RAYMOND J.	TEC 5	INF
ANDERSON, ARTHUR	TEC 4	INF
ANDERSON, JONATHAN E.	2 LT	INF
ARNOLD, J. B.	PVT	AMD
BAILEY, ROBERT H.	PVT	AMD
BENTLEY, WILLIAM W. SR	TEC 4	INF
BERKEBILE, HOMER C.	TEC 5	AMD
BERNARD, EARNEST C.	PVT	AMD
BINTER, JOSEPH F.	1/SGT	AMD

BLUME, LEONARD L.	TEC 4	INF
BOGGS, EWING B.	TEC 4	INF
BRADLEY, WILLIAM J.	PFC	INF
BROOKS, LOWELL H.	CPL	INF
CHERNICK, NICHOLAS JR	SGT	INF
CLARK, EDWARD H.	PVT	INF
CONNELLY, ARTHUR M.	PVT	INF
DANIELO, JAMES L.	PFC	INF
DAVIS, GEORGE H. SR	PVT	INF
DE CRAENE, C.L. JR	1 LT	INF
DE DOMENICI, FRANK	PFC	AMD
DENNISON, LYNN N.	1 LT	INF
DEPASCALE, HERMAN	CPL	INF
DERENSIS, EARNEST	PVT	AMD
DINGELDINE, JESS F.	CPL	INF
DONNELLY, JAMES P. JR	1 LT	CAV
DOUBLEMAN, NATHAN B.	SGT	AMD
DUFF, ALBERT A.	CPL	INF
DUNN, TIMOTHY J.	S/SGT	AMD
ELKINS, JAMES W.	CPL	AMD
ELLIS, GEORGE L. JR	PFC	INF
FARESE, JAMES N.	2 LT	NO
FEDERICO, JOHN A.	CPL	INF
FERRUZZI, VINCENT A.	TEC 5	INF
FESMIRE, GEORGE R.	PVT	AMD
FETT, WILLIAM	PFC	INF
FIBRANZ, CHARLES T.	CPL	AMD
FINCH, EVERETT T.	S/SGT	MD
FURLOW, JOHN H.	PVT	INF
GELAZELA, JOSEPH A.	PVT	AMD
GINOLI, ANGELO	CPL	INF
GNATOWSKI, LEO J.	CPL	AMD
GRIFFITHS, ROBERT J.	TEC 5	INF

GULLETT, FREDERICK A.	PVT	AMD
HAGEMEISTER, JAMES E.	1 SGT	INF
HAMANN, RALPH H.	PVT	INF
HAMMERSCHMIDT, W. H.	PVT	INF
HARDESTY, CARL H.	TEC 5	AMD
HARRIS, MARION L.	1 LT	CAV
HAWK, ROBERT T.	TEC 5	AMD
HAY, RUSSELL J.	PVT	INF
HELLINGS, JOHN F.	1 LT	INF
HILLENBURG, OLLEN	PVT	INF
HOFFMAN, HARLOD P.	CPL	INF
HORBELT, HARRY F.	CPL	INF
HOURN, MICHAEL	SGT	INF
HUMMEL, EARNEST L.	TEC 5	INF
JACKSON, HENRY Y.	PVT	AMD
JEANDHEUR, FRED C.	2 LT	INF
JERSKY, DANIEL	PVT	INF
JOHNSON, HENRY E.	PVT	INF
KAPLIN, WALTER P.	S/SGT	INF
KELLEY, LLOYD J.	TEC 5	AMD
KRASSNER, MATTHEW M.	SGT	INF
LAWSON, JAMES E.	PVT	INF
LERTCHER, EDWARD O.	SGT	AMD
LEVIN, FRANK	PVT	AMD
LEWIS, JAMES T.	PVT	AMD
LIESE, BERNARD	1 LT	INF
LINER, ROBERT B.	TEC 4	INF
LOCKWOOD, FREDERICK F.	2 LT	INF
MANCINI, PHILLIP R.	TEC 4	AMD
MC CLOSKEY, WILLIAM T	PFC	AMD
MC CREER, CHARLES R.	PVT	INF
MC CULLOCH, JESSE M.	TEC 5	INF
MC GUIRE, EDWARD M.	CPL	INF

MC HALE, JOHN J.	SGT	AMD
MCEVEY, PATRICK J.	TEC 5	INF
MCVICKER, WILLIAM J.	PFC	INF
MOORE, CHARLES J.	CPL	INF
MOORE, GEORGE C.	PVT	INF
MORRIS, ROBERT E.	PFC	INF
MULIERI, VICTOR	TEC 5	INF
MURPHY, JAMES G.	PVT	AMD
MYERS, EARL R.	PVT	AMD
NARDIELLO, ANTHONY	CPL	INF
OLINICK, JOHN	TEC 4	INF
OLIVER, BENJAMIN H.	PFC	AMD
PALMER, RUSSELL E.	PVT	INF
PARISH, CLAUDE E.	TEC 4	INF
PARKS, JOHN H.	SGT	INF
PARSONS, ODELL	TEC 4	INF
PECK, LESTER H.	TEC 5	INF
PESHEK, JOHN O,	PFC	INF
PIELAK, STANLEY F.	2 LT	INF
POLITO, ANTHONY V.	PVT	INF
POORE, MAX	1 LT	CAV
POPOVITCH, GEORGE	PFC	INF
PORTER, JERRY J.	PVT	INF
PREVATTE, TRUMAN H.	SGT	AMD
PROFFITT, RAYMOND S.	TEC 5	AMD
RADLAUER, EARL S.	SGT	INF
RATLIFF, WILFRED A.	PFC	INF
RAY, ROBERT F.	PFC	INF
RITLAND, EARNEST O.	SGT	AMD
ROELFS, HARM A.	PVT	INF
ROSS, JOSEPH M.	PVT	AMD
SADDLEMIRE, ALFRED G.	CPL	AMD
SADOWSKI, JOSEPH J.	SGT	INF

SEDLAK, JOSEPH R.	PFC	INF
SHAFER, CLIFFORD R.	TEC 4	AMD
SHUHNICKI, ANTHONY A.	PVT	INF
SIMMONS, WILLIAM G.	PFC	AMD
SIMO, JOHN P.	PFC	INF
SLAUGHTER, MAX J.	PVT	INF
SMITH, DALE F.	CAP	INF
SMITH, FRED L.	PVT	INF
SMITH, HOWARD L. JR	2 LT	NO
SMITH, JOE S.	TEC 5	MD
SOLA, PHILLIP	SGT	INF
SPINA, JOSEPH	SGT	INF
SU SAVAGE, BERNARD J.	1 LT	CAV
SUTINEN, EINO A.	TEC 4	INF
TAYLOR, JOSEPH W.	PFC	INF
TEEPLE, RICHARD H.	PFC	INF
THOMPSON, ROBERT L.	PVT	INF
TROVER, CHARLES U.	CAP	CAV
TUCHINSKY, BERNARD	PVT	AMD
ULIVARRI, DANIEL B.	PFC	INF
VAN KIRK, WILLIAM A.	PVT	INF
VOLK, WILLIAM	CPL	INF
WEINSTEIN, HAROLD	TEC 3	MD
WENRICH, CONRAD T.	CPL	INF
WENTZEL, RAY W.	PFC	AMD
WHITESIDE, JAMES A.	SGT	INF
WISNESKI, SIGMUND	CPL	INF
WOELFLE, EDWARD F.	2 LT	INF
WOLFF, HARRY W.	PVT	AMD
WRIGHT, BERT C.	TEC 5	INF

HQ CO 4TH ARMD TRAIN

CRUSER, CURTIS R.	PVT	INF
NEWTON, ALEXANDER C.	MAJ	INF
ROCK, PAUL M.	SGT	INF
ROGERS, HAROLD B.	PFC	INF

46TH ARMD MED BN

BARTOL, THEODORE J.	TEC 5	MD
ENGLEHUTT, F. A.	TEC 4	MD
KIELKOWSKI, STANLEY W.	PVT	MD
KUTENITS, WILLIAM G.	PVT	MD
MC ARTHUR, JACK L.	PVT	MD

Taps
Rev. Jack G. Amon

"Day is done
Gone the sun
From the hills,
From the plains,
From the skies
All is well-safely rest –
God is nigh!"

Truth and Honor lay dying
On the German Iron Cross;
The whole world reeled in confusion
At freedom's greatest loss.

Then the Fourth Armored Division
Struck like lightening again and again.
The enemy reeled and wondered,
Where, or how, or when.

Only ten-thousand men strong,
Yet like mighty waves on a beach
They lived in endless motion
Filling every weakened breach.

When the 101 Airborne was surrounded
And asked to surrender or die,
Germany's elite was astounded
By their final ""NUTS!" reply.

Then through that frozen ring of fire
The mighty Fourth Armored came
With renewed faith and hope
Setting Liberty aflame.

No greater love has ever had
Such a fine and noble end
When men will lay down life
To save a helpless friend.

And now as life's shadows
Lengthen and start to fall
We, your sons and daughters,
Thank you one and all.

We revere your fallen comrades
Who marched on muted feet
To see the face of God
And know his blessings sweet

You gave to our weary world
The words it longed to hear:
"Victory and Honor!"
And you wrote it plain and clear.

So to that final sunrise
We'll march as friend with friend
To tread those golden highways
Where life will have no end.

Tribute to the Fourth Armored Division
By: Hez H. Ray & Ann Ray Winker